A Generation Under Siege

"Exposing the spirit of Jezebel 's modern day strategy against our youth"

Robert Summers

A Generation Under Siege
"Exposing the spirit of Jezebel 's modern day strategy against our youth" ©

Published by
Summers Ministries
2024

Printed in the USA

ISBN: 9798340629203

Preface

In a time when the world is more connected than ever, we find ourselves witnessing the unraveling of a generation—a generation under siege. Through the rise of social media, entertainment, secular ideologies, and the breakdown of the family unit, today's youth are bombarded with influences that subtly, and sometimes overtly, erode their sense of identity, purpose, and need for spiritual grounding. This is no accident. Behind the scenes, a treacherous and dark force is at work: the Jezebel spirit.

This book, "*A Generation Under Siege*" is my attempt to sound the alarm. I have watched as the enemy has shifted his strategies, no longer confined to the obvious or traditional vices but now operating within the very systems that shape our youth. From the addiction to real time video games that desensitize to violence, to music and media that glorify rebellion, promiscuity, and vanity, to educational systems that strip away moral and spiritual truth, to dysfunctional families —these are the modern-day weapons of the Jezebel spirit. Yet, the battle is not lost.

This is a book call to parents, caregivers and leaders to get serious about faith and spiritual warfare. It is about exposing Jezebel's schemes, understanding how she operates through various cultural and societal mechanisms, and ultimately equipping parents, leaders, and youth to stand firm against this widespread spirit. In these pages, we will explore how Jezebel targets the family, the mind, and the heart—attacking through emotional wounds, dysfunctional families, and misguided societal norms. But more than that, we will delve into some of the practical solutions. Through biblical wisdom, deliverance and prophetic ministry, and applying some practical strategies, we can fight back and break the strongholds that seek to bind this generation.

It is not enough to be aware; we must act, and we must act now. The youth of today are the leaders of tomorrow, and they are being targeted with unprecedented intensity. But with the truth of God's word and the power of spiritual warfare, we can lead them to victory, restoring their God-given identity and purpose.

This book is not just a call to awareness, but a call to action. The time is now—because this generation, under siege, cannot afford to wait.

Table of Contents

Introduction

In every era, children and youth face challenges unique to their time, but the trials faced by today's generation are unprecedented. The rapid rise of technology, the breakdown of the nuclear family unit, and the normalization of moral relativism have created an environment where the most vulnerable are left unprotected. Beneath these societal shifts lies a much deeper spiritual crisis—one rooted in the ancient biblical figure of Jezebel, whose influence represents rebellion, manipulation, and destruction. This spirit, far from being a relic of the past, is alive and active today, subtly infiltrating our homes, schools, and even our churches.

"A Generation Under Siege" is a call to awaken to the spiritual warfare happening right before our eyes. The Jezebel spirit is working methodically to undermine our youth's faith, identity, and future. By using modern tools such as social media, music, entertainment, and education, this spirit entices and ensnares young minds, drawing them away from godly values and leading them into a cycle of confusion, rebellion, and brokenness. The Jezebel spirit thrives in a secular world where instant gratification, fame, and self-promotion overshadow the deeper truths of character, purpose, and faith in God.

This book not only exposes the many ways the Jezebel spirit operates but also highlights how it capitalizes on the emotional, spiritual, and psychological wounds of children. Whether through trauma, abuse, rejection, or dysfunctional family dynamics, the spirit seizes opportunities to control and manipulate. The enemy knows that capturing the hearts and minds of the youth means sowing seeds of destruction that will impact future generations.

"A Generation Under Siege" aims to equip parents, caretakers, and spiritual leaders with the insight and spiritual tools necessary to wage warfare against Jezebel's influence by thoroughly examining these modern-day tactics. We will explore how social media fosters comparison and vanity, how popular music glorifies rebellion and immorality, how video games desensitize young minds to violence, how dysfunctional families are Jezebel's early entry point, and how educational systems, stripped of moral absolutes, leave a spiritual void. More importantly, this book offers strategies for protecting our youth through spiritual guidance, biblical teaching, and active, intentional parenting.

The stakes could not be higher. Our children are not only the leaders of tomorrow but also the battleground where the enemy has launched an all-out assault. It is time to take a stand, not just for the physical well-being of our youth but for their souls. In a world where Jezebel's influence is pervasive, this book serves as both a light in the darkness and a battle plan for spiritual warfare. It is time to rise up and protect this generation from the siege they face.

This is more than just a battle for culture—it is a battle for the future.

Why we wrote this book

The primary goal of this book is to shed light on the devastating impact of the Jezebel spirit on today's youth. We aim to reveal how this ancient spiritual force has embedded itself within modern societal structures, subtly influencing young minds through various systems and cultural trends. In doing so, we hope to raise awareness and provide a deeper understanding of how this spiritual principality operates in our world today.

8

Moreover, our mission is to educate and equip parents, church leaders, Christian counselors, and others with the necessary tools to identify the destructive traits and widespread influence of the Jezebel spirit. This book will provide insight into the spiritual warfare needed to confront and eradicate its grip on the next generation. We will explore how social influences such as media, technology, and dysfunctional family dynamics become gateways for Jezebel's attacks on children and youth.

We will also highlight the crucial role of proper spiritual guidance, strong family values, and an awareness of Jezebel's tactics in combating this pervasive spirit. By better understanding these principles, readers will be adequately equipped to engage in the spiritual battle necessary to protect and nurture the next generation.

While this book does not cover every facet of the Jezebel spirit, it serves as a foundational resource for addressing the many challenges today's youth face. We believe it will be a valuable tool for those committed to understanding and countering Jezebel's influence. For more in-depth resources and discussions on the Jezebel spirit, we encourage you to explore our other writings listed at the end of this book.

Chapter One
Understanding Queen Jezebel and the Spirit of Jezebel

Jezebel in the Old Testament - 1 Kings 16-21, 2 Kings 9

In the Old Testament, Jezebel first appears in 1 Kings 16 when she marries King Ahab of Israel. Jezebel was a Phoenician princess, the daughter of Ethbaal, king of the Sidonians, and a devoted worshipper and high priest of the false god Baal. When she married Ahab, Jezebel introduced the worship of Baal and Asherah into Israel, leading the nation into widespread idolatry, perversion, witchcraft, and rebellion against God. The story of Jezebel is a vivid example of her destructive nature and demonstrates how she became synonymous with evil, control, manipulation, intimidation, perversion, and corruption.

Now Ahab the son of Omri did evil in the sight of the Lord, more than all who were before him. And it came to pass, as though it had been a trivial thing for him to walk in the sins of Jeroboam the son of Nebat, that he took as wife Jezebel the daughter of Ethbaal, king of the Sidonians; and he went and served Baal and worshiped him. Then he set up an altar for Baal in the temple of Baal, which he had built in Samaria. And Ahab made a wooden image. Ahab did more to provoke the Lord God of Israel to anger than all the kings of Israel who were before him – I Kings 16:30-33

Key Features of Jezebel's Life and Wicked Activities

The Promotion of Idolatry
And as if it had been a light thing for him to walk in the sins of Jeroboam...he (Ahab) took for his wife Jezebel......and went and served Baal and worshiped him. 1 Kings 16:31-33

Jezebel was a devoted worshiper of Baal and Asherah, the pagan gods of her native land. After seducing King Ahab into marriage,

Jezebel used her position as queen to aggressively promote these pagan deities in Israel. Under Jezebel's guidance, Ahab erected altars for Baal and permitted idol worship to spread throughout the nation. This provoked God's wrath, as it turned the Israelites away from worshiping Jehovah and into apostasy, whoredom, perversion, and spiritual harlotry.

The Persecution of God's Prophets

Jezebel was notorious for her ruthless persecution of the prophets of God. She sought to systematically eliminate those who spoke on behalf of Jehovah by having them persecuted or killed. Obadiah, a servant of Ahab, was compelled to hide 100 prophets in caves to protect them from Jezebel's wrath.

For it was so, when Jezebel cut off the prophets of the Lord, that Obadiah took a hundred prophets, and hid them by fifty in a cave, and fed them with bread and water -1 Kings 18:4

Jezebel's most famous clash was with the prophet Elijah, who challenged Jezebel's 450 prophets of Baal and 400 prophets of Asherah to a showdown on Mount Carmel.

Now therefore send, and gather to me all Israel unto mount Carmel, and the prophets of Baal four hundred and fifty, and the prophets of the groves four hundred, which eat at Jezebel's table - 1 Kings 18:19

The Murder of Naboth

One of Jezebel's most scandalous acts of manipulation was her role in the murder of Naboth, a righteous Israelite who owned a vineyard that King Ahab desired. When Naboth refused to sell his vineyard to Ahab because it was part of his family inheritance, Ahab became distraught and depressed. So, Jezebel devised a wicked plan. She forged letters in King Ahab's name, accusing Naboth of talking evil of the king, and ultimately had him executed. This act of manipulation and injustice revealed her willingness to use lies, deception, and murder to achieve her objectives.

And she wrote letters in Ahab's name, sealed them with his seal, and sent the letters to the elders and the nobles who were dwelling in the city with Naboth. She wrote in the letters, saying, Proclaim a fast, and seat Naboth with high honor among the people; and seat two men, scoundrels, before him to bear witness against him, saying, "You have blasphemed God and the king." Then take him out, and stone him, that he may die.
- 1 Kings 21:8-10

Spiritual and Political Corruption

There was never anyone like Ahab, who sold himself to do evil in the eyes of the Lord, urged on by Jezebel his wife - 1 Kings 21:25

Jezebel's influence over her husband, Ahab, extended far beyond idolatry and persecution. She also played a significant role in Israel's overall political corruption. Under her influence, Ahab led Israel deeper into sin, which ultimately brought judgment upon the nation of Israel. To contend with this evil, God sent the prophet Elijah to declare judgment on Ahab and Jezebel for their wicked sins. Elijah prophesied that Jezebel would suffer a gruesome death and that dogs would eat her flesh.

And concerning Jezebel the Lord also spoke, saying, 'The dogs shall eat Jezebel by the wall of Jezreel - 1 Kings 21:23

Sexual Immorality

Although not explicitly detailed in scripture, the idolatrous worship of Baal often involved perverse sexual practices such as ritual prostitution, where temple prostitutes engaged in sexual acts as a form of worship to their pagan gods. These rituals were performed in the context of religious festivals and involved sexual activities intended to honor the pagan deity and ensure the fertility of the land and people. Such rites were often conducted in temples and groves dedicated to Baal.

Many rituals included behaviors that led to sexual frenzy, orgies, sodomy, homosexual and pedophilia.

Jezebel's actions paved the way for much spiritual and moral decay in Israel.

Jezebel's Deception and Witchcraft

Jezebel's painting of her face, as described in the Bible, is significant. Jezebel painting her face is not just a physical act but a deeply symbolic sign that reflects her vanity, pride, and malicious deception. Jezebel's use of cosmetics has come to symbolize deception and moral corruption.

Now when Jehu had come to Jezreel, Jezebel heard of it; and she put paint on her eyes and adorned her head, and looked through a window – 2 Kings 9:30

Jezebel painting her face is not just a physical act but a profoundly symbolic gesture that exposes her witchcraft.

> *Now it happened, when Joram saw Jehu, that he said, "Is it peace, Jehu?" So he answered, "What peace, as long as the harlotries of your mother Jezebel and her witchcraft are so many?" –*
> *2 Kings 9:22*

Jezebel's Threats and Intimidation

After Jezebel is informed of the defeat and slaughter of her prophets, she becomes furious. In response, she sent a messenger to Elijah with a death threat.

> *"May the gods deal with me, be it ever so severely, if by this time tomorrow I do not make your life like that of one of them"* - 1 Kings 19:2

Despite Elijah's earlier display of great power, faith, and courage in challenging and defeating the prophets of Baal, Jezebel's threat struck fear into Elijah's mind. Rather than standing firm and trusting in God, the mighty prophet Elijah was overcome by fear and ran for his life. He went to Beersheba, a remote town in Judah, and left his servant there.

Elijah's Despair

Elijah continued into the wilderness, traveling alone and deeply depressed. He eventually settled under a tree and prayed for death.

"I have had enough, Lord," he said. "Take my life; I am no better than my ancestors" - 1 Kings 19:4

Elijah was overwhelmed by his fear. Despite the astonishing victory at Mount Carmel, he believed that his efforts were in vain, having not produced any change, particularly regarding Israel's apostasy under the influence of Jezebel and Ahab.

Elijah's fear of Jezebel's imminent wrath drove him to hide in a cave. In the cave, God spoke to him, asking:

"What are you doing here, Elijah?" - 1 Kings 19:9

Elijah replied by expressing his deep discouragement. He explained that despite his zealous efforts to serve God, the Israelites had rejected the covenant, torn down God's altars, and killed His prophets.

"I have been very zealous for the Lord God Almighty. The Israelites have rejected your covenant, torn down your altars, and put your prophets to death with the sword. I am the only one left, and now they are trying to kill me too. - 1 Kings 19:10

Ultimately, God gave Elijah specific instructions on what to do. He was to anoint Jehu as king over Israel and Elisha as his successor as prophet

The Lord said to him, "Go back the way you came, and go to the Desert of Damascus. When you get there, anoint Hazael king over Aram. [16] Also, anoint Jehu son of Nimshi king over Israel, and anoint

Elisha son of Shaphat from Abel Meholah to succeed you as prophet.
- 1 Kings 19:15-16

These actions ultimately led to the downfall of Ahab's reign and Jezebel's eventual judgment.

Jezebel's Death

Jezebel's demise came when Jehu, anointed by the prophet Elisha to be king of Israel, was sent by God to execute judgment on the house of Ahab. When Jehu came to Jezreel, Jezebel attempted to confront him, but her servants tossed her out of a window at his command.

Now when Jehu had come to Jezreel, Jezebel heard of it; and she put paint on her eyes and adorned her head and looked through a window. Then, as Jehu entered at the gate, she said, "Is it peace, Zimri, murderer of your master?" And he looked up at the window, and said, "Who is on my side? Who?" So, two or three eunuchs looked out at him. Then he said, "Throw her down." So, they threw her down, and some of her blood spattered on the wall and on the horses; and he trampled her underfoot. - 2 Kings 9:30-33

Then, as prophesied by Elijah, dogs consumed her body, leaving only her skull, feet, and hands. This horrible death served as a vivid example of divine judgment and vengeance for Jezebel's evil deeds.

This is the word of the Lord that he spoke by his servant Elijah the Tishbite: In the territory of Jezreel the dogs shall eat the flesh of Jezebel, and the corpse of Jezebel shall be as dung on the face of the field in the territory of Jezreel, so that no one can say, This is Jezebel
- *2 Kings 9:36-37*

Jezebel's Legacy

Jezebel is historically infamous for her defiant rebellion against Jehovah, her ruthless manipulation of power, and her role in leading Israel into witchcraft, perversion, and idolatry. In modern times, the term "Jezebel spirit" is often used to describe the same destructive forces she embodied—idolatry, control, manipulation, intimidation, seduction, and the erosion of spiritual and moral values, along with the loss of one's true identity. Throughout scripture, Jezebel stands as a stark warning of the devastating consequences of aligning with such treachery, perversion, and rebellion against the Kingdom of God.

Though Queen Jezebel is long gone, the demonic force linked to her, known as the "Jezebel spirit," continues its relentless assault on individuals, children, families, and nations alike.

Today, Jezebel's demonic legacy remains evident, manifesting in various ways throughout modern society.

Introducing the Jezebel Spirit: A Biblical Perspective

The Jezebel spirit, though not explicitly named as such in Scripture, is drawn from the characteristics and actions of Queen Jezebel, the historical figure from the Old Testament, and the spiritual warning of her characteristics seen in the 1st-century church. Jezebel's influence represents not only an individual's evil actions but also a pervasive spirit of control, manipulation, perversion, witchcraft, and dysfunction. This ancient insidious spirit is especially dangerous to children and teenagers, who are highly impressionable and vulnerable to Jezebel's influence.

As previously mentioned, Jezebel is one of the most infamous women in the Bible. Her story is a vibrant example of the destructive influence of idolatry, manipulation, and spiritual rebellion. Her name alone is synonymous with narcissism, control, and moral corruption.

The idea that the "spirit of Jezebel" persists, even though Queen Jezebel died (approximately 834 B.C.), comes from a spiritual interpretation rather than a literal one. In Christianity, Jezebel is often seen as more than just a historical figure or the name of a popular women's publication. Her actions and influence in the Bible, particularly her manipulation, idolatry, control, and rebellion against God, have come to symbolize a specific type of spiritual oppression or influence that still exists today.

When someone refers to the "spirit of Jezebel," they are often referring to a demonic influence that operates in the same way that the literal Queen Jezebel did. It represents rebellion, pride, idolatry, sexual immorality, corruption, control, manipulation, intimidation, and the destruction of families, which persists today.

The "spirit of Jezebel" is a type of demonic force or influence that seeks to corrupt, control, and lead people away from God and His divine order, especially by preying on the insecure, rejected, wounded, abused, depressed, traumatized, and rebellious. This demonic influence is believed to operate through systems, cultures, races, families, and individuals. Jezebel is a sophisticated, highly intelligent demonic principality that has built a complete network designed to keep humanity in bondage to Satan and the kingdom of darkness.

The spirit of Jezebel manifests today in various ways, especially in aspects of modern culture, such as through manipulation, sexual

19

immorality, idolatry (whether worldly or spiritual), and destructive behaviors. The Jezebel spirit is a 'breeder' of cycles of dysfunction that plague many families and society at large.

In short, while Jezebel as a person is long gone, the "spirit of Jezebel" is metaphorically used for the tenacious, destructive influence that aligns with what Jezebel represented in the Bible.

The Jezebel Spirit in the New Testament

"Yet I have this against you: You are permitting that woman Jezebel, who calls herself a prophetess, to teach my servants that sex sin is not a serious matter; she urges them to practice immorality and to eat meat that has been sacrificed to idols. I gave her time to change her mind and attitude, but she refused. Pay attention now to what I am saying: I will lay her upon a sickbed of intense affliction, along with all her immoral followers, unless they turn again to me, repenting of their sin with her and I will strike her children dead. And all the churches shall know that I am he who searches deep within men's hearts, and minds; I will give to each of you whatever you deserve. – Revelation 2:20-24 (The Living Bible)

In the New Testament, the Jezebel spirit reappears, not as an individual but as a spiritual influence within the church. In Revelation 2:20, Jesus rebukes the church in Thyatira for tolerating "that woman Jezebel, who calls herself a prophetess," and leads His servants into sexual immorality and idolatry.

Here, Jezebel is not a historical figure but a symbol or type of the same spiritual manipulation, control, and perversion that marked her actions in the Old Testament.

As can be seen, the church in Thyatira was complacent, having most likely been seduced by the spirit operating in some people. Some of the indicators of the Jezebel spirit in Thyatira were:

False Teachings

Just as Jezebel in the Old Testament lured Israel into idolatry and false worship, manipulating power and corrupting the nation's spiritual integrity, the Jezebel spirit in Thyatira similarly infiltrated the early church, seducing believers with false teachings. This spirit encouraged not only sexual immorality but also led them to partake in practices forbidden by God, such as consuming food sacrificed to idols. Distorting biblical truths undermined the spiritual foundation of the church, promoting a lifestyle of compromise and rebellion against God's commands. This parallels the way Jezebel's influence in ancient Israel blurred the lines between devotion to God and the worship of false deities, bringing destruction and moral decay to those who followed her ways. Both then and now, the Jezebel spirit seeks to entice believers away from true worship and lead them into spiritual corruption under the guise of freedom and enlightenment.

Deception of the Vulnerable

The Jezebel spirit preys on God's people, with a particular focus on new believers and vulnerable children. By exploiting their spiritual immaturity, emotional wounds, and lack of discernment, this spirit draws them into sin and wickedness, often masquerading as a source of enlightenment or self-empowerment. Its influence is subtle yet destructive, planting seeds of doubt, rebellion, and confusion that gradually pull them away from God's truth and moral foundations.

The Jezebel spirit is relentless, not only seeking to corrupt individuals but also destabilizing entire churches. It uses vulnerable members to sow division, confusion, and moral decay, weakening the collective spiritual growth of the church and creating an atmosphere ripe for manipulation, compromise, and rebellion.

Tolerance for Evil

Jesus sternly rebuked the church in Thyatira in Revelation 2:20:

"Nevertheless, I have this against you: You tolerate that woman Jezebel, who calls herself a prophet. By her teaching she misleads my servants into sexual immorality and the eating of food sacrificed to idols."

This sharp warning highlights how dangerous it is to tolerate the Jezebel spirit, which can easily infiltrate leaders and believers alike when it is not confronted appropriately. The church in Thyatira allowed false teachings to take root, leading many astray, and this demonstrates how critical it is to maintain vigilance and discernment in spiritual matters.

Athaliah, the evil daughter of Jezebel

Jezebel's influence did not end with her death. Her children continued in the same path of idolatry and rebellion against God. Her daughter Athaliah, for example, reigned in Judah and continued in the same wickedness. The story of Athaliah helps us to understand the generational impact the spirit of Jezebel can have.

Athaliah, the daughter of Jezebel and King Ahab demonstrates a compelling example of how the spirit of Jezebel works through manipulation, control, and the destruction of family lineage, especially when it comes to the attack on children. Athaliah's life provides a dynamic parallel to the spirit of Jezebel's attacks on youth today.

Now when Athaliah the mother of Ahaziah saw that her son was dead, she arose and destroyed all the royal family. But Jehosheba, the daughter of King Joram, sister of Ahaziah, took Joash the son of Ahaziah and stole him away from among the king's sons who were being put to death ...... 2 Kings 11:1-2

In 2 Kings 11, Athaliah usurps the throne of Judah after her son, King Ahaziah, is killed. To secure her power, she orders the massacre of all royal heirs, including her grandchildren. This brutal act of murder highlights several key themes that link to the modern-day spiritual attack against children being explored in this book.

The Destruction of Legacy and Destiny

Athaliah's brutal massacre of her own family was a calculated attempt to destroy the Davidic line, through which the Messiah was prophesied to come. Her goal was not just to secure her power but to obliterate any hope of a future challenger by erasing the royal bloodline.

Today, this same destructive spirit undermines our youth's spiritual inheritance, seeking to prevent future generations from entering the Kingdom of God and walking in the fullness of their God-given destiny. It aims to sever the legacy of faith and purpose, leaving children and young people disconnected from their true identity in

Christ. This spirit is also evident in the modern-day abortion movement, where the lives of the innocent are taken, and entire families and races are threatened with extermination. Its goal remains the same: to cut off life, destiny, and the continuation of God's plan for future generations.

Massacre as a Symbol of Rejection and Trauma

Athaliah's ruthless slaughter of her own family members can be seen as a symbol of deep betrayal and rejection. The children she murdered were not only physically abused but were also rejected by the very person meant to protect and nurture them. This mirrors the way children today often experience trauma, abuse, and rejection, which are central access points for the spirit of Jezebel.

Today, the spirit of Jezebel can operate through broken family systems, abuse, or abandonment, where children feel rejected by those meant to care for them, leading to emotional and spiritual wounds that persist well into adulthood.

Usurping Authority and Control

Athaliah's actions represent the spirit of Jezebel's desire for total control, including the control over the next generation. By killing her grandchildren, she usurped authority over Judah and attempted to establish a reign of tyranny. Similarly, the spirit of Jezebel in today's context seeks to control and manipulate children through various societal and spiritual influences, shaping their worldview and behavior in ways that serve destructive agendas.

In today's world, bullying and intense peer pressure to conform, the rise of occult practices, media influences, and even certain educational trends can be seen as attempts by the spirit of Jezebel to control the minds and hearts of children, steering them away from Kingdom truth and righteousness.

Jehoiada's Role as a Protector of the Next Generation

Athaliah's massacre was ultimately spoiled when Jehoiada, the priest, and his wife saved the infant Joash, hiding him in the temple for six years until he could be restored to his rightful position as king. This highlights the critical importance of spiritual leadership and protection in safeguarding the next generation. Jehoiada's actions symbolize the role of parents, spiritual leaders, and the Church at large in shielding our youth from the Jezebel spirit's influence and supporting their spiritual growth and awareness.

Today, parents, teachers, mentors, and spiritual leaders need to aggressively stand against the forces of evil trying to destroy the next generation.

The Legacy of Jezebel in Generational Sin

Athaliah's actions vividly illustrate how the destructive influence of the Jezebel spirit can extend across generations. Just as Jezebel manipulated Israel into idolatry and rebellion, her daughter Athaliah carried on this legacy of evil through murder and a relentless pursuit of control. This generational influence mirrors the cycles of dysfunction, trauma, and abuse that often repeat within families, leaving children vulnerable to Jezebel's destructive forces.

These generational patterns are clearly visible today. Broken families, unresolved trauma, and emotional wounds create fertile ground for spiritual and emotional strongholds that specifically target children and youth. The Jezebel spirit preys on these vulnerabilities, using them to perpetuate cycles of pain, rebellion, and destruction. Recognizing and breaking these cycles is crucial for freeing future generations from the grip of the Jezebel spirit and enabling them to walk in their God-given destiny.

The Jezebel spirit is not merely a relic of the past but a present-day force, actively targeting youth to destroy their spiritual inheritance, potential, and future. It aims to cut off their connection to God, derail their purpose, and rob them of the fullness of life and destiny God has prepared for them. Breaking these chains and restoring families to wholeness is crucial in releasing future generations from Jezebel's influence and empowering them to live out their divine calling.

Conclusion

In understanding Queen Jezebel and the spirit associated with her, it becomes clear that this is not just a historical figure or an isolated biblical story. Jezebel's legacy continues to influence and manipulate in subtle yet powerful ways, targeting individuals, families, and entire societies. Her methods of control, seduction, idolatry, and rebellion are still in operation today, working to corrupt spiritual and moral values, particularly among the vulnerable and the youth. Recognizing the tactics of the Jezebel spirit is the first step in resisting its influence. Armed with spiritual discernment, prayer, and the truth of God's Word, we can stand against this destructive force, reclaiming our identity in Christ and protecting future generations from its grip. By breaking these strongholds, we open the way for God's kingdom to flourish, restoring spiritual inheritance and releasing people into the fullness of their divine purpose.

Chapter Two
Jezebel's Exploitation of Youth

In this chapter, we examine the numerous ways the Jezebel spirit exploits a child's life, beginning from birth and continuing through adolescence. From the very start, children are highly vulnerable to emotional wounds, trauma, rejection, and dysfunction within their families. These formative experiences create openings for the Jezebel spirit to exploit, manipulate, and distort the child's perception of themselves, others, and even God. Understanding how Jezebel targets these vulnerabilities provides valuable insight into how this spirit takes root and thrives in a child's life.

The Jezebel spirit is relentless in its exploitation of trauma and emotional pain, using these as entry points to gain control over a child's mind and heart. It thrives in the chaos of broken families, where emotional neglect, abuse, and the absence of moral and spiritual guidance are common. In these dysfunctional environments, Jezebel works to exploit the confusion, rebellion, hopelessness, and despair that surfaces, distorting the child's sense of identity and purpose.

As children grow, they remain particularly susceptible to Jezebel's exploitation, especially during the critical stage of identity formation. The spirit capitalizes on early experiences of neglect and rejection to fracture the emotional and spiritual well-being of the child. Through various gateways—including secular media, toxic cultural norms, peer pressure, and a corrupted educational system—the Jezebel spirit gains deeper influence. Whether it's through the desensitizing effects of violent media, the seductive pull of the occult, or the normalization of false ideologies, Jezebel subtly but effectively exploits these areas to erode a child's moral foundation and spiritual connection to God.

Furthermore, the Jezebel spirit employs manipulative and controlling tactics, exploiting the emotional instability of children to bind them in cycles of fear, rebellion, and dependence—cycles that often persist into adulthood. These exploitative patterns of control leave deep emotional scars and spiritual confusion, trapping children in cycles of shame and spiritual bondage. By examining how Jezebel systematically weaves deception and instability into a child's life, this chapter reveals how deeply entrenched this spirit becomes, creating a lasting impact that can follow children for years if not generations.

Our goal is to expose these exploitative tactics, showing how Jezebel works to undermine a child's future by breaking down their spiritual resilience and emotional strength. Recognizing and understanding these patterns is the first step in countering the destructive influence of the Jezebel spirit and reclaiming a child's destiny in God.

Trauma

Trauma, particularly during formative years, deeply affects a child's emotional, mental, and spiritual development. From birth, a child who experiences neglect, violence, or chaotic environments may develop a heightened sense of fear and insecurity. This opens the door for the Jezebel spirit to manipulate that fear, often manifesting as confusion, distrust, and an inability to form healthy attachments and relationships.

There are 4 main ways the Jezebel spirit uses the gateway of trauma to infiltrate a child's life. They are:

- Severe Rejection
- Molestation or Rape
- Emotional abuse
- Physical abuse

Whether newborns, infants, toddlers, preschool, school age, or adolescents, trauma, such as being exposed to unstable environments or emotional abandonment, can create a deep sense of insecurity. Children usually internalize trauma even when they cannot articulate it, leading to emotional and psychological wounds that fester over time.

As children grow into their adolescent years, the effects of unhealed trauma can manifest as rebellion, isolation, or seeking validation in unhealthy ways. The Jezebel spirit takes advantage of this by luring children into self-destructive behaviors, often by manipulating their unmet emotional needs and desires for control over their lives.

Rejection

Rejection is more than just an emotional event. It can also manifest as a demonic spirit that seeks to attack and oppress children, mainly targeting their identity, security, and self-worth. Rejection is a spirit often employed by Jezebel to isolate a person from their creator God. This spirit also seeks to distort a person's perception of themselves, causing them to believe they are unworthy, unloved, or unwanted.

The spirit of rejection works by introducing lies in children's minds, telling them they are not good enough and that their parents and family members do not love or accept them. These lies are reinforced through dysfunctional patterns in the family, such as broken relationships, neglect, abuse, or betrayal, making a child more vulnerable to feelings of worthlessness and isolation. As these feelings take root, the spirit of rejection can cause strongholds in a child's mind, influencing their behavior and leading them into further emotional disconnection and spiritual bondage.

In children, the spirit of rejection can take hold early, particularly if they grow up in dysfunctional family environments where they feel unloved, neglected, or compared unfavorably to others, especially siblings. This influence can shape their identity in destructive ways, leading them away from their true purpose, spiritually and earthly.

Rejection from parents, peers, or society—creates wounds that the Jezebel spirit will exploit. Children who feel rejected are likelier to internalize and entertain the enemy's lies about their worth and purpose, believing they are unlovable, inadequate, and don't measure up. This creates a deeply rooted fear of abandonment and rejection, driving them to seek affirmation and control in unhealthy ways.

There are two primary forms of rejection that can profoundly impact a child: fear of rejection and self-rejection.

Fear of rejection arises when a child experiences the pain of being dismissed or devalued by others. This fear often takes root early, shaping how they view relationships and their worth in the eyes of others. As they internalize this fear, they begin to anticipate rejection, avoiding vulnerability and connection to shield themselves from further hurt.

Self-rejection, on the other hand, develops when a child's mind becomes conditioned to believe that they are inherently unworthy of love and acceptance. Over time, they view themselves as flawed or shameful, blaming themselves for the lack of love and affirmation in their lives. This belief system often stems from unmet emotional needs—such as love, validation, attention, support, correction, and training—from the people they rely on the most: parents, siblings, and close caregivers.

When a child's fundamental need for love and acceptance goes unfulfilled, it creates a gaping doorway for the Jezebel spirit to enter. This spirit thrives in environments where rejection is prevalent, using the deep wounds of unfulfilled emotional needs to manipulate and control, further entrenching the child in patterns of fear, insecurity, and self-doubt.

Words of Rejection

Rejection is often expressed through words. The words of a mother and Father matter the most in a child's life. From infancy, a child's perception of themselves and their world is shaped by their interactions with their parents. Words spoken by parents form the core of a child's self-esteem and emotional health. Positive affirmations such as *"I love you," "You're important,"* and *"You can do it"* promote a sense of security and worth. Positive words support a child's growth and confidence, while negative words can have detrimental effects.

There is immense power in our words. They can either bring life or death to situations and relationships. With children, parents and leaders should always speak words that edify and encourage, being mindful of how our words affect and shape children.

The word of God expresses the importance of speaking positive, kind, and loving words.

"The tongue has the power of life and death, and those who love it will eat its fruit." - Proverbs 18:21

"Do not let any unwholesome talk come out of your mouths, but only what is helpful for building others up according to their needs, that it may benefit those who listen." - *Ephesians 4:29*

"A gentle answer turns away wrath, but a harsh word stirs up anger." - Proverbs 15:1

"Let your conversation be always full of grace, seasoned with salt, so that you may know how to answer everyone." - Colossians 4:6

Even while in the womb, words spoken around or about a child have a profound impact, opening doors for demonic influence. Spirits of rejection can enter a child's life even before birth through the negative and harmful words released into their environment. When parents or others shout, belittle, use profanity, or release damaging speech around children, they unwittingly grant Jezebel the authority to establish a stronghold in that child's life.

The Jezebel spirit capitalizes on these negative words, deepening the child's sense of rejection and unworthiness. By amplifying feelings of inadequacy, failure, or being unloved, Jezebel further isolates the child emotionally, encouraging them to pull away from healthy relationships. As a result, the child begins seeking validation and acceptance from unhealthy, often destructive sources.

Children are particularly vulnerable to internalizing negative words and absorbing the harmful messages directed at or around them. This internalization leaves them more susceptible to the manipulative tactics of the Jezebel spirit, which exploits their insecurities and deep-seated rejection to assert control. Over time, the child becomes trapped in a cycle of manipulation, shaped by the negative words they've internalized, and the emotional wounds left unhealed.

The Need for Healing

"He heals the brokenhearted and binds up their wounds." Psalm
147:3

Addressing the impact of negative words is critical for both emotional and spiritual healing. It not only involves restoring a child's emotional well-being but also breaking the stronghold of the Jezebel spirit that feeds off rejection and insecurity. Providing consistent positive communication and affirmation is essential for rebuilding a child's self-worth and resilience.

To reverse the damage caused by harmful words, it is crucial to replace negativity with positive reinforcement. Affirming a child through encouraging words, genuine praise, and expressions of love helps restore their sense of value and identity. These words act as a healing balm, counteracting the deep wounds inflicted by past criticism and promoting a healthy self-image.

Moreover, fostering healthy and supportive relationships is vital in helping children overcome the harmful effects of toxic speech. By encouraging open communication, emotional support, and trust, children can find a safe space to heal and develop resilience against Jezebel's manipulative influences. Parents, leaders, and caregivers play a vital role in this process, as their consistent love and support are instrumental in undoing the effects of the destructive words spoken over a child's life.

Below are some practical ways to reverse the damage done through word curses hurled at children:

Affirmation and Encouragement

Children who have faced harsh criticism need ongoing affirmation to restore their self-esteem. It is essential for parents and leaders to consistently speak words of love, encouragement, and belief in the child's potential. By affirming their strengths, talents, and inherent worth, we can help heal the wounds left by past criticism. It is important to remind the child that their value is not tied to perfection or accomplishments but to who they are at their core. They are fearfully and wonderfully made in the image of God, reflecting His likeness, which makes them invaluable. Reminding children of this truth can help them see that their worth is rooted in their identity as God's highest creation, not in meeting others' expectations or achieving success.

Exhibiting Positive Self-Talk

Children internalize negative criticism and develop harmful self-talk. Parents and leaders can teach them to replace negative thoughts with positive ones by exhibiting healthy self-talk themselves. Helping children be aware of and challenge negative thoughts is crucial. Teach them phrases like, "*I can do all things through Christ who strengthens me*," or "*nothing is impossible.*'

When they make mistakes, don't speak negatively towards them or start yelling and punishing them. Instead, remind them that everyone learns through failure and encourage them to embrace it, interpreting it as part of their growth and development journey.

Finally, regularly saying, "*I believe in you*," or "*You are loved just as you are*," can have a powerful healing effect.

Create a Safe-Supportive Environment

We are all shaped by two key factors: our DNA and our environment. While our genetics determine our physical resemblance to our parents, the environment we are raised in plays a vital role in shaping who we become. Environments saturated with harsh and critical words can stifle a child's ability to express themselves and create a deep fear of making mistakes. This fear can hinder their growth and development, both emotionally and spiritually.

To nurture a child's growth, parents and leaders must create an environment where children feel safe and secure—where they can take risks, make decisions, and learn from their mistakes without the fear of harsh judgment. Feedback focusing on improvement and growth rather than criticism fosters emotional intelligence and self-confidence. In such a supportive environment, children are less likely to fall under the manipulative influence of the Jezebel spirit as they grow in strength, security, and resilience.

Forgiveness

Critical words can deeply wound a child, leaving lasting emotional scars. Teaching children the power of forgiveness toward others and themselves helps them release these burdens and move forward with emotional freedom. It's essential to explain that holding onto unforgiveness harms the one carrying it more than it affects the person who caused the hurt. Parents and leaders must model this by practicing forgiveness in their own lives.

Unforgiveness often leads to bitterness, which acts like a toxic poison, affecting both the mind and body. The Jezebel spirit thrives in bitterness, using it to create turmoil within a child's heart, clouding their judgment and inviting emotional and physical distress. Many illnesses and diseases are linked to the bitterness and resentment that come from unforgiveness, making it crucial for parents and leaders to teach and model the freedom found in forgiving.

"For I see that you are poisoned by bitterness and bound by iniquity." – Acts 8:23

"Watch out that no poisonous root of bitterness grows up to trouble you, corrupting many." – Hebrews 12:15(b)

Praying and Speaking the Word

Prayer is undeniably a powerful tool for healing the wounds left by past criticism. Parents and leaders can pray specifically for emotional healing, protection, and restoring a child's confidence and identity in Christ. Rather than allowing negative words (curses) to take root, speaking blessings reinforces the child's sense of worth and purpose in God's plan. Declaring affirmations over their identity, potential, and future is essential to undoing the damage Jezebel may have inflicted.

Fathers, in particular, are uniquely responsible for speaking blessings over their children. By consistently laying hands on them and imparting the love of God into their hearts and minds, they can strengthen their children spiritually and emotionally. A profound example of this is found in Scripture with Jacob, who, nearing the end of his life, gathered his sons and grandsons to speak blessings over each of them. His act of imparting spiritual inheritance and love serves as a powerful model for fathers today to follow, ensuring that their children grow in strength, security, and God's favor.

By faith Jacob, when he was dying, blessed each of the sons of Joseph, and worshiped, leaning on the top of his staff. - Hebrews 11:21

The Impact of Family Rejection

When a child experiences rejection from parents or caregivers, the impact can be profound and long-lasting, often resulting in attachment disorders that carry into adulthood. These attachment issues can make it difficult for the child to trust others or feel safe and secure in relationships. As they grow, the inability to form healthy emotional bonds may lead to struggles with intimacy, connection, and vulnerability, causing a cycle of relational dysfunction that persists over time.

Rejection within the family can also promote a deep sense of emotional abandonment. When a child feels unloved or unwanted by those who should be their greatest source of care and security, they may internalize feelings of inadequacy, believing they are unworthy of love and acceptance. This emotional void can be fertile ground for the spirit of Jezebel to take root. Jezebel seeks to amplify these wounds of rejection, intensifying the child's feelings of abandonment, insecurity, and unworthiness.

As a result, the child may begin seeking validation through destructive behaviors, trying to fill the emotional void with external sources of comfort—whether through unhealthy relationships, substance abuse, or seeking approval from the wrong people. This pattern of seeking validation from harmful sources only deepens their emotional wounds as they drift further from the love, security, and acceptance they genuinely need.

In addition, the Jezebel spirit often influences the child to internalize their pain and rejection, encouraging them to adopt controlling or manipulative behaviors as a means of self-preservation. Having been hurt and rejected, they may unconsciously believe that taking control of relationships or situations is the only way to protect themselves from further emotional harm. This manipulation, however, only mirrors the very rejection they experienced and perpetuates a cycle of unhealthy, toxic interactions.

Ultimately, the child may grow into adulthood, struggling with deep-seated trust issues, emotional instability, and a propensity to engage in or attract toxic, controlling relationships. Understanding these dynamics is crucial, as breaking the cycle of rejection and healing the wounds caused by it can prevent Jezebel's influence from taking hold and restore the child's ability to form healthy, loving, and secure relationships.

Developing a Sense of Worthlessness

Rejection from family can deeply wound a child's sense of self, often leading to feelings of worthlessness and inadequacy. When children are denied the unconditional love and acceptance they crave from their family, they internalize this rejection, believing that they are inherently unworthy of love. This emotional pain makes them more vulnerable to external influences that promise validation, acceptance, or a sense of "fitting in", even if those sources are destructive or manipulative.

Rejection from one's family of origin damages a child's self-esteem and disrupts the healthy attachment patterns necessary for forming quality relationships later in life. When a child is denied emotional safety and stability within their family, they struggle to build trust, establish healthy boundaries, and maintain intimate connections. This relational instability creates an emotional void, leaving the child more likely to seek out unhealthy people or toxic behaviors in an attempt to fill that emptiness.

The Jezebel spirit preys on these feelings of rejection, using them to create a stronghold in the child's life. As the child becomes more desperate for love and validation, Jezebel manipulates this emotional vulnerability, leading them toward relationships, ideologies, or behaviors that promise fulfillment but ultimately bring harm. Whether it's through toxic friendships, addictive behaviors, or destructive patterns of seeking approval, the child's need for support can be exploited, further isolating them from healthy sources of support.

Furthermore, rejection disrupts the foundation of a child's emotional and spiritual well-being, making them more susceptible to the manipulative exploitation by others. A child who has experienced rejection may struggle with feelings of uncertainty and a lack of self-worth, which can be easily exploited by those with controlling or harmful intentions. This makes them a prime target for manipulative spirits like Jezebel, who seeks to dominate and control through emotional instability.

Over time, this cycle of rejection and manipulation can erode the child's ability to trust others and build healthy relationships. Without intervention and healing, these patterns may continue into adulthood, affecting their capacity for intimacy, security, and emotional resilience.

Breaking this cycle requires emotional healing and spiritual deliverance, restoring the child's sense of significance and helping them form healthy, compassionate relationships that reinforce their true identity as loved and valued.

Emotional Vulnerability

The spirit of Jezebel is a disruptive force characterized by manipulation and control. When it comes to influencing children, especially those who have experienced family rejection or emotional wounds, the spirit of Jezebel can use emotional vulnerabilities within a child to influence them and take them down a dark path in life.

The spirit of Jezebel seeks to make children vulnerable to its negative and toxic exploits by targeting their most formative years when their sense of identity, values, and beliefs are still being formed. Children who experience rejection, trauma, or emotional neglect are particularly vulnerable to the Jezebel spirit. This insidious spirit capitalizes on insecurities and emotional wounds, whispering lies about their self-worth, identity, and future. By planting seeds of self-doubt, inferiority, and rejection, the Jezebel spirit can embed itself in a child's mind, distorting their perception of themselves, others, and their world. Children who feel rejected may also struggle with low self-esteem, anxiety, and depression, thus creating an emotional vacuum that the Jezebel spirit can exploit.

Spiritual Implications

Rejection can create a spiritual opening where dark-demonic forces, like the spirit of Jezebel, find a foothold. The child's emotional and psychological wounds make them more susceptible to manipulation and control. The emotional wound of rejection can open the door for a demonic spirit of rejection to take root in a child's life.

Remember that the spirit of rejection feeds on past hurts and magnifies them, often leading the child to believe that others will always reject or abandon them. As such, the child may experience spiritual oppression, where the spirit of rejection continually feeds lies about their value and place in the world. This can manifest in feelings of despair, isolation, self-hatred, and even rebellion as the child attempts to cope with or defend against further rejection.

Rejection makes children susceptible to deception, leading them away from the truth of the gospel and into spiritual confusion. The Jezebel spirit and other demonic influences can use this vulnerability to lure children into practices or beliefs that are harmful and spiritually dangerous.

Seeking Attention and Validation

In the absence of family support, children might seek validation and attention from external sources, including harmful influences. The spirit of Jezebel might exploit this need, offering a counterfeit sense of acceptance or power. Children who feel neglected or misunderstood may become vulnerable to the lure of gangs and alternative lifestyles that promise protection, acceptance, and identity. Gangs often provide a false sense of family, filling the emotional void created by dysfunctional homes or absent parents. Children are drawn into these groups because they crave attention and acceptance, making them easy targets for Jezebel's manipulation and control.

Low Self-Esteem

Rejection can lead to feelings of low self-worth. The spirit of Jezebel may manipulate these feelings by creating situations where the child feels they are only valuable or loved when they meet certain demands or conditions.

The spirit of Jezebel will capitalize on a child's low self-esteem to create a pattern of people-pleasing and co-dependent behavior. Children with low self-worth often seek validation from others, making them easy targets for Jezebel's manipulation. The Jezebel spirit exploits this weakness by instilling a fear of rejection, driving the child to seek approval at any cost, often sacrificing their own needs or boundaries. To counter the pain of rejection, a child may develop into a "people-pleaser." As people-pleasers, children may become overly accommodating, fear confrontation, and be unable to stand up for themselves, leading them into toxic relationships.

Developing Co-dependent Behavior

The Jezebel spirit promotes co-dependence by teaching the rejected child that their value is derived from how much they can do for others, creating a cycle of constant striving for acceptance and love but never feeling worthy. This pattern can carry into adulthood, making it difficult for the person to form healthy, balanced relationships, as they constantly look outward for validation instead of developing inner confidence and spiritual identity.

The spirit of Jezebel takes advantage of a child's experiences of rejection and a dysfunctional family environment, leading to the development of co-dependent behaviors. The Jezebel spirit thrives on emotional instability generated from rejection, promoting the need to constantly seek validation and support from others to fill the emotional gap created by the dysfunctional family environment. Children who experience rejection or emotional manipulation in their family of origin can become excessively compliant to the desires of others, forfeiting their own needs to receive approval. They may take on the role of the "fixer," trying to stabilize their dysfunctional family dynamics by being the one who meets everyone else's needs. This behavior is a key indicator of co-dependency, and it trains the child to believe that love is earned through what they do for others.

As they mature, these co-dependent behaviors manifest in romantic relationships, friendships, and work environments. The now-grown child may find it challenging to set boundaries or stand up for themselves, fearing that doing so will result in rejection, abandonment, and being discarded. This leads to a turbulent cycle of unhealthy, lopsided relationships where they always give without receiving. Often, this leads to becoming emotionally drained, manipulated, or taken advantage of. This also allows the Jezebel spirit to manipulate them through guilt, fear of rejection, shame, and the constant need for approval.

Development of Narcissistic Behavior

Rejection often creates a deep sense of inadequacy and insecurity in children, leaving them emotionally vulnerable. To cope with the pain of rejection, children may develop defense mechanisms to protect themselves, one of which can be the development of narcissistic traits. This overcompensation arises from their perceived lack of worth as they attempt to mask their feelings of insecurity by projecting an inflated sense of self-importance.

Children who experience emotional instability may also develop a heightened need to control their environment or the people around them. This desire for control is a coping mechanism, helping them manage their internal chaos and lack of stability. The spirit of Jezebel preys on this vulnerability, encouraging the child to exert control in unhealthy ways. Often, this manifests as manipulative behaviors, where the child may resort to bullying or abusing others to feel powerful and secure.

Through this manipulation and control, Jezebel tightens its grip on the child's life, reinforcing patterns of dominance and emotional abuse. Rather than addressing their pain, the child is led deeper into destructive behaviors, further entrenching the spirit's influence. This cycle of control, manipulation, and dominance becomes a barrier to healing, making it critical to address both the emotional wounds and the spiritual strongholds at play. By controlling the child's actions through shame, guilt, fear, or promises of reward, the spirit of Jezebel ensures that the child behaves in ways that serve its agenda. This might involve encouraging deceitful behavior (chronic lying), manipulation of others, or even self-destructive actions.

The wounded child may begin to focus excessively on self-promotion and superiority to disguise their feelings of rejection and shame. The Jezebel spirit takes advantage of this dynamic by encouraging the child to adopt behaviors that elevate themselves above others—traits often associated with narcissism—such as an inflated sense of self-importance, a constant craving for praise, and a lack of empathy.

As the child matures into adulthood, these narcissistic tendencies can severely impact their ability to connect with others. They may prioritize their own needs and desires at the expense of others, leading to a lack of empathy. As the narcissistic-Jezebelic spirit takes root, the child may view relationships as transactional rather than reciprocal. Over time, they will develop a habit of using others to get what they want, with no regard for the feelings or needs of those around them. The Jezebel spirit enhances this manipulation by nurturing a false sense of superiority, making it difficult for the child to recognize their shortcomings.

Children who develop narcissistic behaviors influenced by the Jezebel spirit may gravitate to positions of power or influence, believing that their worth is tied to their ability to control others. Often, they misuse authority, seeing it as a means to validate their self-importance rather than as an opportunity to minister to others. This can cause much damage in ministries, churches, or communities of faith, where narcissistic leadership can lead to manipulation, corruption, perversion, and deception.

Undermining Authority

The spirit of Jezebel might work to undermine the child's respect for legitimate authority figures, such as parents or teachers. By persuading the child that these figures are untrustworthy or harmful, the spirit positions itself as the alternative source of guidance and control.

The Jezebel spirit may exploit any pre-existing tension between the child and their parents in dysfunctional households. If the child feels ignored or misunderstood, the spirit can amplify feelings of rejection, leading them to reject and rebel against their parents' authority. As the child progresses through the education system, they may behave disrespectfully toward teachers, viewing them as oppressive rather than supportive.

Over time, this contempt for authority often leads to horrible consequences. A child who consistently rejects legitimate authority may struggle with discipline, self-control, and accountability. These issues can manifest in poor academic performance, strained relationships, and behavioral problems that, if left unchecked, will be used by Jezebel to bring destruction and continue the generational dysfunction.

Peer Rejection in Adolescence

As children grow into adolescence, peer rejection can further fuel feelings of insecurity. The Jezebel spirit may manifest through the pressure to fit into destructive peer groups, engage in sexual immorality, or experiment with dangerous behaviors in a bid to gain acceptance. Peer rejection, especially during adolescence years, can dramatically shape a child's sense of self and worldview. Repeated rejection by peers can cause deep emotional wounds.

When a child is consistently rejected by their peers, they may begin to believe Jezebelic lies such as *"I am unworthy," "I am defective,"* or *"I'm insignificant."*

To compensate, the child may start seeking acceptance in places that entangle them in demonic bondage. The Jezebel spirit influences the child to look for affirmation in external sources such as inappropriate friendships, toxic relationships, gangs, or harmful subcultures that exploit their need for belonging. This pursuit of acceptance often leads the child to adopt behaviors, attitudes, and belief systems that go against the nature of God and Kingdom values. This is one of the reasons teenagers engage in sex, drugs, alcohol, and other lascivious behavior.

When a child faces peer rejection, the Jezebel spirit often introduces feelings of shame and guilt, not only for the rejection itself but also for the child's reaction to it. The child might feel ashamed for not fitting in. The spirit of Jezebel uses peer rejection to isolate the child from positive influences further, making them even more susceptible to the spiritual attack of Jezebel.

Molestation

The spirit of Jezebel is an insidious spirit that wants to bring extensive harm to a child's life. Its ruthless attack on innocent children comes in many forms. One of the ways Jezebel disrupts a person's life is through molestation and rape.

Molestation refers to the act of subjecting a child or vulnerable individual to inappropriate and harmful sexual contact or behavior. This can involve any physical, emotional, or verbal actions of a sexual nature that are intended to exploit or harm the victim. Molestation is a form of sexual abuse that significantly impacts the emotional and psychological well-being of the victim. Molestation includes a range of sexual activities that are demonic and highly inappropriate for children. This can include touching, fondling, language, and exhibiting behavior that is sexual in nature.

Examples of Molestation may include:

- Physical Contact: Inappropriate touching, fondling, or other forms of physical contact that are sexual in nature. This may include Sexual Intercourse and Oral copulation

- Sexual Advances: Making sexual comments, suggestions, or advances towards a child or vulnerable person.

- Exposure to Sexual Material: Forcing or coercing a child to read or view explicit sexual material or participate in sexual acts.

- Sexual Exploitation: Any form of sexual activity intended for the gratification of the perpetrator involving a child or vulnerable person.

- Sexual Exhibitionism: Showing one's genitals or private areas to children and unwanted parties.

Molestation often occurs in environments where there is a natural trust, such as within families, schools, or religious institutions. This breach of trust intensifies the trauma experienced by the victim. Child molestation inflicts profound trauma on a child. This abuse can lead to deep-seated feelings of shame, guilt, and confusion. The trauma disrupts the child's sense of safety and self-worth, creating fertile ground for further manipulation by the Jezebel spirit.

The psychological impact of molestation includes anxiety, depression, and trust issues. Children who have been molested often struggle with forming healthy relationships and may experience persistent fear or hyper-vigilance.

The emotional impact of molestation on children is intense and, many times, long-lasting, affecting multiple areas of emotional development. Children who have experienced molestation may struggle with:

Shame and Guilt

The Jezebel spirit exploits the shame and guilt associated with molestation. It magnifies these feelings, making the child believe they are at fault or unworthy of love and protection. This exploitation further isolates the child and makes them more susceptible to manipulation.

The spirit of Jezebel uses the shame stemming from the molestation to maintain control over the child's thoughts and actions. This control can manifest as spiritual bondage, where the child feels trapped in a cycle of negative beliefs and destructive behaviors.

The spirit can use the trauma of molestation to instill a sense of helplessness and self-loathing in the child. By reinforcing these feelings, Jezebel ensures the child remains emotionally and spiritually bound, creating a cycle of dysfunction. The spirit of Jezebel will lie to children, telling them that they are to blame for what happened, either because they were manipulated into thinking so by the molester or because they believe they should have done something to stop the abuse.

Fear, Anxiety, and Distrust

The Jezebel spirit uses the trauma from molestation to instill fear and distrust in relatives, authority figures, and other caregivers. Children may begin viewing all relationships as potentially harmful, reinforcing their sense of isolation and dependence on the spirit's manipulation.

Children may become frightened of certain people, places, or situations that remind them of the abuse. This anxiety can manifest as fear of being hurt again, fear of being judged or disbelieved, or even a generalized fear of trusting others.

Creating Dysfunction and Spiritual Bondage

The Jezebel spirit often drives a child toward self-destructive behaviors as a way of coping with the emotional pain and trauma caused by molestation. This can manifest in various harmful behaviors, such as substance abuse, self-harm, promiscuity, or seeking out unhealthy and toxic relationships. These destructive patterns only serve further to entrap the child in a cycle of dysfunction, deepening the emotional and spiritual damage inflicted by Jezebel.

One of the ways Jezebel tightens its hold is through spiritual bondage in the form of trauma bonding. Trauma bonding occurs when a person becomes emotionally attached to someone through repeated cycles of abuse or trauma. In the case of a child, this bond may form with an abusive caregiver, friends, or others who perpetuate the trauma. Jezebel uses this dynamic to keep the child trapped in toxic relationships, drawn to people who either share similar traumas or are likely to inflict further harm. This unhealthy attachment prevents healing and keeps the child in a constant state of emotional vulnerability, reinforcing the cycle of pain and control orchestrated by Jezebel.

Sexual Confusion and Dysfunction

Molestation, particularly when experienced at a young age, can create profound confusion about sexuality. The trauma of abuse distorts a child's understanding of sex and intimacy, often linking it with fear, pain, and manipulation. As they grow older, these distorted views can manifest in various harmful ways, including sexual dysfunction and toxic behaviors.

Victims may struggle with an inability to form healthy, intimate connections or develop hypersexuality as a way to cope with unresolved trauma. Other potential consequences include confusion about gender identity, a loss of libido, compulsive behaviors such as chronic masturbation or self-gratification, or difficulty maintaining healthy boundaries in relationships. In some cases, the trauma may even contribute to struggles with same-sex attraction or behaviors, all rooted in the confusion and emotional damage caused by the spirit of Jezebel. These patterns can further complicate the child's ability to develop a healthy sense of self and engage in fulfilling relationships later in life.

Post-Traumatic Stress Disorder (PTSD)

Children who experience molestation are at high risk of developing symptoms of Post-Traumatic Stress Disorder (PTSD), which can significantly impact their emotional and psychological well-being. These symptoms may include vivid flashbacks in which the child relives the trauma as though it is happening again, often triggered by specific people, places, or situations that remind them of the abuse. Nightmares and intrusive thoughts are also common, disrupting sleep and making it difficult for the child to feel safe, even in their own mind.

In an attempt to cope with the overwhelming pain, many children may emotionally "numb" themselves, a response known as emotional anesthetizing. This coping mechanism allows them to detach from their feelings, but it often leads to difficulties in processing emotions and forming deep, meaningful connections with others. Over time, the child may struggle with regulating their emotions, vacillating between intense anger, sadness, or fear, and periods of complete emotional withdrawal.

Avoidance behaviors are another hallmark of PTSD in children. They may go to great lengths to avoid people, places, or activities that remind them of the abuse, withdrawing from social interactions or activities they once enjoyed. This avoidance can isolate them further, limiting their ability to form trusting relationships or engage in normal developmental experiences. The combination of reliving the trauma, emotional numbness, and avoidance creates a cycle of distress that can profoundly affect the child's overall development and ability to heal from the abuse.

Isolation and Disassociation

To cope with the pain from the abuse, some children may dissociate and detach from their feelings or even from reality to protect themselves from further harm. Children may also shut down emotionally, becoming numb to their feelings and experiences, which can prevent them from processing their trauma and healing from it.

Additionally, Jezebel will deploy demons of worthlessness and shame in an attempt to isolate the child from supportive relationships. This isolation makes it easier for the spirit to maintain control and deepen the child's spiritual bondage. The Jezebel spirit strategically uses isolation as a powerful tool to gain control over vulnerable children and youth. Isolation creates an environment where emotional and spiritual manipulation can occur more easily because the child becomes disconnected from positive people. By isolating the child from healthy relationships and support systems, the spirit creates an emotional and spiritual void where it can plant seeds of fear, insecurity, and confusion.

Distortion of Identity

The Jezebel spirit actively works to distort a child's sense of identity, causing them to see themselves through the broken lens of their trauma rather than through the truth of who they are in God. This spiritual manipulation twists their perception of self, often leading them to believe that their worth is defined by the pain, abuse, or rejection they have endured. As a result, they may develop a deeply skewed self-image, seeing themselves as damaged, unworthy, or even unlovable.

This distortion of identity doesn't just affect their self-esteem; it also creates a disconnection from their true spiritual identity. Rather than recognizing themselves as beloved children of God, made in His image and filled with divine purpose, the child begins to internalize the lies of Jezebel, believing that their trauma defines them. This spiritual disconnection can lead to feelings of hopelessness, isolation, and confusion as the child struggles to reconcile their worth with the false narratives imposed by the spirit of Jezebel.

Over time, this distorted identity can manifest in a range of destructive behaviors—self-sabotage, unhealthy relationships, or even rejection of their own identity and purpose. They may feel disconnected from God, finding it difficult to trust Him or believe in His love, mercy, and healing. In essence, Jezebel seeks to rob the child of their divine inheritance, replacing it with a counterfeit identity rooted in pain and brokenness.

Restoring a child's sense of true identity requires breaking the spiritual and emotional chains imposed by Jezebel, helping them see themselves not through the lens of trauma but through the lens of God's love, grace, and purpose. By reconnecting with their true spiritual identity, they can begin to heal, rebuild their self-worth, and walk in the fullness of who they were created to be.

Abuse

Abuse—whether physical, emotional, or verbal—creates a fertile ground for the spirit of Jezebel to take root and establish a stronghold in a child's life. The trauma inflicted through abuse cuts deep into the heart and mind, leaving the child with profound wounds that can shape their sense of self and the world around them. These deep emotional scars often manifest as shame, anger, and confusion, distorting their view of authority, love, and trust.

The shame caused by abuse can be particularly crippling. Rather than recognizing that the abuse is not their fault, children often internalize the experience, believing there must be something inherently wrong with them to have been treated this way. This toxic belief system creates a sense of unworthiness and inadequacy, making the child more susceptible to the manipulative influence of Jezebel, which thrives on feelings of rejection and shame.

Abuse also breeds anger—anger at the abuser, at the lack of protection, and often at themselves for feeling powerless. This unresolved anger can fester, turning into bitterness or rage, which Jezebel uses to manipulate the child further. The child may struggle to form healthy relationships, viewing authority figures with suspicion or resentment, as the abuse has warped their understanding of what love and authority should look like.

Confusion compounds the damage as the child grapples with mixed messages about love, safety, and trust. When those who should provide care and protection become the source of pain, the child's ability to discern genuine love from manipulation becomes blurred. Jezebel capitalizes on this confusion, using it to twist the child's perception of relationships and authority, making it difficult for them to trust or feel secure in healthy, loving environments.

Over time, these wounds can form a stronghold, allowing Jezebel to continue its influence into adulthood, manifesting as dysfunctional relationships, mistrust of authority, and a distorted understanding of self-worth. Healing from this type of abuse requires not only addressing the emotional and psychological wounds but also breaking the spiritual chains that Jezebel has placed on the child's life. By exposing the roots of this stronghold, the process of restoration can begin, allowing the child to regain their true sense of identity and experience healthy, loving relationships free from the manipulative influence of Jezebel.

Emotional abuse

Emotional abuse is a toxic pattern of behavior by parents, caregivers, or significant adults that systematically undermines a child's emotional well-being and hinders their healthy development. In dysfunctional families, this type of abuse often involves a consistent use of harmful verbal and non-verbal interactions that erode a child's self-esteem, sense of security, and mental health. Emotional abuse is deeply toxic and creates a major gateway for the Jezebel spirit to gain access to a child's life.

This abuse can take many forms, including persistent criticism, belittling, threats, and derogatory language directed at the child. Such harmful words and behaviors wear down the child's sense of self-worth, leading them to believe that they are inadequate or unlovable. Emotional abuse also manifests through neglect—ignoring the child's emotional needs, withholding affection, or failing to provide the support and care they require. This lack of responsiveness to a child's feelings creates a void where the spirit of Jezebel can begin to sow seeds of insecurity and rejection.

Another insidious form of emotional abuse involves using guilt, shame, intimidation, or manipulation to control the child's emotions and behavior. This can include making the child feel responsible for family problems or using them to meet the parent's emotional needs. Such behavior is narcissistic, abusive, and a hallmark of the Jezebel spirit, which thrives on controlling and manipulating vulnerable individuals.

Unpredictable or erratic emotional responses from caregivers further destabilize the child, creating an environment of confusion and instability. This might include outbursts of anger followed by periods of neglect or even moments of praise—creating a "push-pull" dynamic often seen in relationships influenced by Jezebel's narcissistic tactics. Children raised in this chaotic environment become highly susceptible to Jezebel's manipulative attacks as they struggle to find emotional stability and self-worth.

Frequently dismissing or invalidating a child's emotions only deepens the wounds. Telling a child, they are overreacting, that their feelings are irrelevant, or that they should not feel the way they do compounds the emotional damage. This behavior leaves the child exposed to Jezebel's arsenal of destructive tools, reinforcing the sense that their emotions and needs do not matter and paving the way for further emotional and spiritual harm.

Jezebelic Impact on Children

Emotional abuse can lead to low self-esteem and a distorted self-image. The child may internalize the negative messages, believing they are unworthy, inadequate, and don't measure up. The child may experience anxiety, depression, and other emotional disorders as a result of constant emotional stress and instability.

Additionally, emotional abuse can inhibit the child's ability to form healthy relationships with other children, schoolmates, and relatives and cause a withdrawal from social interaction with others. This can lead to trust, attachment, and communication issues. Children emotionally abused may also display behavioral problems, including aggression, acting out, and withdrawal as a response to the emotional turmoil and dysfunction.

An emotionally abused child often has difficulty trusting adults and forms a distorted view of what love and authority should be. This lack of trust becomes fertile ground for the spirit of Jezebel to convince the child that power, control, and manipulation are necessary for survival.

Distorted Identity

Abuse often robs children of their true identity, creating feelings of worthlessness and confusion about their purpose. The spirit of Jezebel, which thrives on identity confusion and control, uses this to push the child toward destructive behaviors, unhealthy relationships, or involvement in occultic or rebellious influences.

Once the child's identity is compromised, the spirit of Jezebel begins to shape their emotional and psychological patterns. Jezebel works through wounds such as fear, rejection, anger, and shame and can cause the child to internalize those feelings, leading to an ongoing pattern of emotional instability.

Gender confusion (gender dysmorphia)

The spirit of Jezebel is associated with the distortion of truth. Trauma that originates from the family or origin, close family members, or authority figures such as daycare workers, schoolteachers, and spiritual leaders such as Pastors, Priests, and Bishops can influence a child's development, especially in formative years. It can severely disrupt their sense of identity. Gender identity, based on God's original intent, is one of the most personal aspects of self-perception. When a child is exposed to trauma—whether through family dysfunction, abuse, or societal pressures—they may struggle to establish a clear and stable understanding of who they are, including their gender.

Children exposed to emotional abuse or rejection often feel disconnected from themselves, leading them to question not just their worth but their very identity. If a child is controlled or manipulated by figures influenced by the spirit of Jezebel, they may be subtly or overtly taught to question their inherent nature, making them more susceptible to confusion about their gender.

Remember, the significant theme in trauma linked to the spirit of Jezebel is rejection. When a child experiences rejection—whether through emotional or verbal abuse, specifically from parental figures they often internalize feelings of worthlessness or self-doubt. These feelings of rejection and shame may cause the child to question different aspects of their identity, including their gender. This internal struggle can manifest as gender dysphoria, where the child feels disconnected from their biological sex. Some children may adopt a different gender identity as a way of coping with feelings of rejection, seeking acceptance, or belonging in other communities or groups. This can be compounded by societal trends or influences that promote fluidity in gender roles and identity.

The spirit of Jezebel is also linked to promoting ideologies that confuse and destabilize traditional values. Social media, entertainment, and educational systems can be viewed as tools used by this spirit to further promote confusion, especially regarding gender. When a child grows up in a society where gender changeability is celebrated or where traditional gender roles are challenged and often under attack, it can further distort their understanding of their gender. This spirit is embedded in modern societal structures in an attempt to normalize and encourage the questioning of biological sex and traditional gender roles and promote a sense of confusion in children already wrestling with trauma.

Technologically, platforms like social media, music, and entertainment often introduce children to ideas about gender changeability. If a child is already dealing with trauma and a disrupted identity, they may be more vulnerable to these external demonic influences.

Spiritual Disconnection and Gender Confusion

A child experiencing trauma influenced by the spirit of Jezebel may also experience a spiritual disconnect, which can contribute to gender dysphoria. A solid spiritual foundation in the Kingdom of God provides a clear sense of identity grounded in divine purpose. Trauma can sever or distort this connection, leaving the child vulnerable to spiritual confusion, including confusion about their gender. Gender dysphoria can be seen as part of the broader spiritual attack on the child's God-given identity, a way in which the enemy seeds confusion to undermine the child's purpose.

The spirit of Jezebel's influence can lead a child to feel disconnected from God's original design for their identity, including gender, which can manifest as dysphoria or confusion about their place in the world.

Dysfunctional family structures, which are often linked to the spirit of Jezebel, play a significant role in shaping a child's understanding of gender roles. Children learn much about gender from observing their parents or caregivers. If they grow up in an environment where gender roles are distorted—whether through controlling behaviors, abusive relationships, or gender rejection—they may struggle to form a healthy understanding of their own gender identity.

If a parent or guardian is also confused about gender roles or is dominated by the spirit of Jezebel, this confusion can be passed down to the child, either directly or indirectly.

The emotional trauma influenced by the spirit of Jezebel can deeply affect a child's sense of self, leading to gender confusion or dysphoria. Through identity disruption, rejection, societal pressures, spiritual disconnect, and dysfunctional family dynamics, this spirit attacks the foundational understanding of identity, leaving children vulnerable to gender confusion.

Dysfunctional Family of Origin

Dysfunctional family environments and unstable homes are fertile ground for Jezebel's spiritual attacks. When children grow up in households marked by substance abuse, broken relationships, emotional instability, or violence, they become prime targets for the Jezebel spirit, which thrives in chaos and confusion. These environments lack the healthy structure and stability that align with the principles of God's Kingdom. Without this foundation, children are often left without the moral compass and clear boundaries they need to succeed in life. In homes where parents are absent, neglectful, or inconsistent in their discipline and care, the Jezebel spirit seizes the opportunity to step in as an alternative influence, further destabilizing the family.

In Genesis 49:4, it is written, "*Unstable as water, thou shalt not excel.*" This Scripture highlights the destructive nature of instability. Dysfunctional homes, with their constant turmoil, are incapable of fostering growth, success, or emotional security for the children within them.

In such families, parents are often entangled in unhealthy behaviors like addiction, violence, or manipulation, becoming toxic role models for their children. The behaviors children observe in these dysfunctional environments become normalized, leading them to either accept or mimic these destructive patterns. The Jezebel spirit capitalizes on this dysfunction, cementing children in cycles of rebellion, disobedience, and unhealthy relationships. For example, children who witness controlling, manipulative, or abusive tendencies in their family of origin may adopt these behaviors as their own, perpetuating Jezebel's influence and passing it on to future generations.

Furthermore, dysfunctional family environments are often devoid of spiritual growth and guidance. This absence of spiritual leadership leaves children disconnected from God and unaware of their divine purpose. A spiritual void is created in homes where prayer, worship, deliverance, and sound biblical teaching are lacking, allowing the Jezebel spirit to operate freely. Without a solid spiritual foundation, children are more vulnerable to secular ideologies, esoteric beliefs, or even occult practices, as they seek answers and identity in all the wrong places. The Jezebel spirit thrives on this spiritual disconnection, steering the child further from God's truth and into a world of deception, lies, and deeper dysfunction.

Ultimately, these environments breed cycles of dysfunction that affect not only the individual child but the family for generations. Without intervention, the Jezebel spirit continues to exert its influence, keeping the family trapped in brokenness, instability, and spiritual disconnection patterns. Only through a return to God's truth, spiritual discipline, and a commitment to breaking these generational strongholds can families escape this destructive cycle and experience true freedom and restoration.

The Impact on Divorce and Separation

When parents' divorce, and even if a child is given up for adoption or placed in a foster home, they may frequently experience deep emotional wounds. The Jezebel spirit can exploit these wounds by magnifying negative emotions such as fear, anger, sadness, and confusion. The child may internalize these feelings, leading to a distorted self-image or unhealthy coping mechanisms. This spirit thrives in environments where there is chaos, emotional instability, and fractured relationships, feeding off the emotional turmoil the child experiences.

The spirit of Jezebel thrives on division and strife. In divorce it often exacerbates the emotional and spiritual rift between parents and children, driving wedges between family members. Children may blame one parent or be caught in the middle of conflicts, and this spirit can fuel resentment, anger, or bitterness that disrupts their ability to form healthy relationships later in life.

In many cases, children of divorced parents struggle with rebellion, rejection, depression, anxiety, or other behavioral disorders. The Jezebel spirit can exploit these challenges, pushing the child toward destructive behaviors like substance abuse, pornography, self-harm, or other addictive tendencies as they try to numb their pain or fill the emotional void left by the broken family unit.

Divorce often disrupts the parental role in the child's life, and this is where Jezebel may try to sever the child's spiritual covering and guidance. By fostering resentment or mistrust toward one or both parents, the spirit weakens the parental authority and leaves children spiritually vulnerable, opening them up to further manipulation by external influences like peers, media, and ungodly ideologies.

Fathers

Contrary to the narrative promoted by modern culture and secular ideologies, it is the father's God-given responsibility to raise and train his children. Fathers play a pivotal role in shaping the spiritual and moral foundation of their families. Beyond simply providing for their physical needs, fathers are called to offer spiritual guidance, instill moral values, and protect and validate their children. A father's role is to set a godly example, modeling Christlike behavior that their children can follow.

According to Scripture, fathers are ordained as the spiritual leaders of their households. They are entrusted with the responsibility of teaching their children about God, nurturing their faith, and cultivating an environment where biblical principles are lived out daily. A father's influence in these areas is critical, as he is called to shepherd his family, guiding them not only in practical matters but also in their walk with the Lord. Fathers are meant to be the cornerstone of spiritual development within the family, ensuring that their children grow up grounded in faith, love, and righteousness.

Here are just a few scriptures that point to the importance of the Fathers (men) operating in what God called them to be and do.

Fathers, do not provoke your children to anger but bring them up in the discipline and instruction of the Lord. – Ephesians 6:4

"These commandments that I give you today are to be on your hearts. Impress them on your children. Talk about them when you sit at home and when you walk along the road, when you lie down and when you get up."- Deuteronomy 6:6-7

"Anyone who does not provide for their relatives, and especially for their own household, has denied the faith and is worse than an unbeliever." – I Timothy 5:8

Train up a child in the way he should go: and when he is old, he will not depart from it. – Proverbs 22:6

Or as the NIV says ……. *"Start children off on the way they should go, and even when they are old they will not turn from it."*

MIA – Missing Fathers

Many fathers are missing in action when it comes to raising a child. In homes where the father fails to take responsibility for his children, the emotional, behavioral, and spiritual foundation of the family is weakened and vulnerable to external influences. The lack of paternal leadership often leaves children without the validation and protection they need. It also opens the door for harmful spiritual forces—such as the Jezebel spirit—to exert their influence and gain a foothold. A father's neglect or absence can set in motion a vicious cycle of emotional wounding, abuse, and spiritual vulnerability, leaving his children to navigate the challenges of life without a secure foundation. This section explores how the father's failure to lead, teach, and raise his children exposes them to destructive Jezebelic influences that hinder emotional and spiritual development.

Effect on daughters

When a father neglects his God-given responsibility to teach, validate, and love his daughter, or if he abandons her altogether, the emotional, behavioral, and spiritual consequences can be profound and far-reaching. A father's presence—or lack thereof—plays a crucial role in shaping a daughter's sense of self-worth, security, and identity. When that foundational relationship is broken or absent, it creates a vacuum in her life that the Jezebel spirit quickly exploits, leading to an array of negative outcomes.

Emotionally, a daughter without a father's love and validation may struggle with feelings of unworthiness, rejection, and abandonment. She may develop deep insecurities and constantly seek external validation to fill the emotional void left by her father. This emotional instability often manifests as low self-esteem, a distorted sense of identity, and an inability to form healthy emotional bonds. The Jezebel spirit thrives in this environment of emotional vulnerability, sowing seeds of confusion, self-doubt, and despair.

Behaviorally, the absence of a healthy father figure can lead a daughter to engage in destructive behaviors as she searches for the love and validation she missed. Without her father's protective guidance and affirmation, she may turn to unhealthy relationships, seeking approval in all the wrong places. This can result in a cycle of toxic relationships, promiscuity, or even rebellion against authority. The Jezebel spirit capitalizes on this behavioral chaos, leading the daughter further down a path of manipulation, control, and dysfunction.

Spiritually, the consequences of a father's absence can be just as severe. A daughter who has not experienced her earthly father's love, care, and guidance may find it difficult to trust or relate to her heavenly Father. This spiritual disconnection leaves her vulnerable to the lies of the Jezebel spirit, which distorts her understanding of love, authority, and her identity in Christ. Instead of embracing her God-given purpose and value, she may be led into deception, relying on counterfeit sources of spiritual fulfillment that only deepen her wounds.

The absence of a father is not just an emotional or physical void—it is a spiritual one as well. Fathers are called the first example of love, protection, and leadership in their daughters' lives. When they fail in this role, the Jezebel spirit steps in to exploit the resulting vulnerabilities, leading to emotional brokenness, behavioral dysfunction, and spiritual disconnection. For a daughter to truly heal and break free from these destructive influences, she needs both the restoration of her relationship with her earthly father and the revelation of her identity in Christ, where she is fully known, loved, and valued.

Emotional Impact

Low Self-Worth and Insecurity – A daughter who grows up without the validation and love of her father often struggles with deep feelings of inadequacy, insecurity, and low self-esteem. The absence of a father's affirmation leaves a significant void, causing her to constantly seek approval from others in an attempt to fill that gap. This emotional vulnerability makes her an easy target for the Jezebel spirit's manipulation, drawing her into toxic relationships or behaviors as she tries to find the validation she lacks. Without healthy boundaries, she may attract people who take advantage of her need for acceptance, reinforcing a cycle of emotional pain and dysfunction.

Fear of Rejection – The lack of a father's active presence can instill a deep-rooted fear of rejection in a daughter. This fear may drive her toward unhealthy attachments, people-pleasing tendencies, or co-dependent relationships, where she sacrifices her own needs in a desperate attempt to keep others from abandoning her. To avoid rejection, she may strive for perfectionism or try to earn love through performance and conformity, believing that she can only hope to be accepted through flawless behavior. The Jezebel spirit amplifies this fear, pushing her further into relationships where she feels she must constantly prove her worth.

Emotional Intimacy – A daughter who grows up without a father's presence may struggle to trust men in her future relationships, fearing they will eventually leave her as well. This leads to difficulties in forming deep emotional intimacy, as she guards her heart to protect herself from further abandonment. The Jezebel spirit fosters the belief that men cannot be relied upon for emotional support, convincing her that she is better off withholding her trust and affection, which can sabotage healthy relationships and isolate her from genuine love.

Behavioral Impact

Rebellion and Disobedience – Without the stabilizing influence of a father's guidance, a daughter may become rebellious toward authority figures, including her mother, teachers, or other adults. This rebellion can manifest in defiance, anger, or outright disobedience, often fueled by the spirit of Leviathan, which thrives on pride and rebellion. The wounded daughter may also gravitate toward peers who engage in negative behaviors, such as substance abuse, promiscuity, or self-destructive acts. Jezebel capitalizes on this rebelliousness, pushing her further into destructive lifestyles and away from the path of healing and wholeness.

Validation Seeking – Daughters who lack fatherly validation often seek male attention in unhealthy ways, which can lead to promiscuity, involvement in toxic relationships, or even prostitution. The desire to feel noticed, loved, or valued drives them to seek out men who exploit rather than support or uplift them. The Jezebel spirit plays on this longing for approval, entangling them in cycles of emotional abuse and manipulation, reinforcing the belief that their worth is tied to male attention and approval.

Avoidance or Overdependence – In response to their father's absence, some daughters may choose to avoid relationships with men altogether, building emotional walls to guard themselves against potential hurt. Others may swing to the opposite extreme, becoming overly dependent on male attention or approval, hoping to fill the void left by their absent father. In either case, the Jezebel spirit exploits these extremes, further distancing the daughter from healthy, balanced relationships.

Additionally, many young women are drawn to emotionally unavailable or toxic men, unconsciously repeating the abandonment patterns they experienced in childhood. Jezebel may convince them they deserve these unhealthy relationships or that this is the best they can hope for. In more extreme cases, a daughter may seek validation through promiscuity or sexual relationships, believing that physical intimacy is the only way to feel loved or valued by men. This reflects Jezebel's influence, manifesting in seduction, immorality, and perversion.

Without a father's affirmation and love, many young girls turn to unhealthy sources for male validation. The Jezebel spirit exploits their emotional and spiritual wounds, steering them toward relationships that only deepen their pain and reinforce feelings of unworthiness. For healing to occur, these destructive cycles must be broken, and the daughter must recognize her inherent value in Christ, apart from the validation of others.

Spiritual Impact

Susceptibility to Jezebel's Influence - Without the father's spiritual covering, leadership, and support, daughters are more susceptible to the Jezebel spirit's manipulations. This spirit preys on emotional wounds and insecurities, often offering false validation through worldly connectivity, vanity, the occult, and rebellion against moral and spiritual principles.

Lack of Spiritual Identity - A father's role in imparting a spiritual identity is crucial. A father's absence often results in a spiritual gap where the daughter struggles to develop a strong relationship with God, leaving her spiritually wandering and susceptible to secular and occult influences.

Biblical Examples:

Dinah, Daughter of Jacob - Dinah was the daughter of Jacob, who appears to have neglected her in some manner. This led her to a volatile situation where she wanted a social connection with women outside her people, resulting in her being taken advantage of. Dinah's story shows the dangers that can arise when a daughter is not adequately protected and guided by her father.

And Dinah the daughter of Leah, which she bare unto Jacob, went out to see the daughters of the land. And when Shechem the son of Hamor the Hivite, prince of the country, saw her, he took her, and lay with her, and defiled her.

And they said, Should he deal with our sister as with a harlot? –
Genesis 34:1-2, 31

Tamar, the daughter of King David - Tamar was a victim of her half-brother Amnon's assault. After he raped his sister, her father, David, failed to properly deal with the situation, leaving her wounded and shamed. David's procrastination and emotional distance as a father reflect how neglect and abandonment can lead to deep emotional and spiritual scars for a daughter.

And it came to pass after this, that Absalom the son of David had a fair sister, whose name was Tamar; and Amnon the son of David loved her. And Amnon was so vexed, that he fell sick for his sister Tamar; for she was a virgin; and Amnon thought it hard for him to do anything to her. But Amnon had a friend, whose name was Jonadab, the son of Shimeah David's brother: and Jonadab was a very subtil man. And he said unto him, Why art thou, being the king's son, lean from day to day? wilt thou not tell me? And Amnon said unto him, I love Tamar, my brother Absalom's sister. And Jonadab said unto him, Lay thee down on thy bed, and make thyself sick: and when thy father cometh to see thee, say unto him, I pray thee, let my sister Tamar come, and give me meat, and dress the meat in my sight, that I may see it, and eat it at her hand. So Amnon lay down, and made himself sick: and when the king was come to see him, Amnon said unto the king, I pray thee, let Tamar my sister come, and make me a couple of cakes in my sight, that I may eat at her hand. Then David sent home to Tamar, saying, Go now to thy brother Amnon's house, and dress him meat. .... Amnon said unto Tamar, Bring the meat into the chamber, that I may eat of thine hand. And Tamar took the cakes which she had made, and brought them into the chamber to Amnon her brother. And when she had brought them unto him to eat, he took hold of her, and said unto her, Come lie with me, my sister. And she answered him, Nay, my brother, do not force me; for no such thing ought to be done in Israel: do not thou this folly. And I, whither shall I cause my shame to go? and as for thee, thou shalt be as one of the fools in Israel. Now therefore, I pray thee, speak unto the king; for he will not withhold me from thee.

Howbeit he would not hearken unto her voice: but, being stronger than she, forced her, and lay with her. - 2 Samuel 13:1-7, 10-14

The Woman at the Well (see John 4:1-26) - Although the Bible doesn't specifically mention her father; clearly, this woman's past relationships suggest she was seeking validation through multiple marriages and relationships. Jesus addressed her deeper need for deliverance and spiritual enlightening, highlighting how the lack of a supporting father can lead to a life of searching for love in all the wrong places.

Effect on sons

Biblically, the role of a father is fundamental in shaping a son's emotional, spiritual, and moral development. A father's presence provides far more than just physical support—it offers emotional security, validation, and a crucial model for godly living. Fathers are called to be both protectors and guides, offering their sons a stable foundation to build their lives. When a father fulfills this God-given role, he instills confidence, teaches resilience, and sets the example for what it means to be a man of integrity, strength, and faith.

However, when this fatherly presence is absent—whether through neglect, abandonment, or disengagement—it creates a significant void in a son's life. Without a father to offer emotional grounding and guidance, the son may struggle with feelings of insecurity, rejection, and confusion. The Jezebel spirit seeks to exploit this void, planting seeds of dysfunction that can manifest in various ways.

Emotionally, sons who grow up without their father's validation often experience a deep sense of inadequacy. They may question their worth, constantly seeking approval from others or striving to prove themselves. This leaves them vulnerable to manipulation and deception as they look for affirmation in unhealthy relationships, behaviors, or achievements. Without the strong identity a father helps establish, the son may become susceptible to the Jezebel spirit's influence, leading him to adopt rebellious, aggressive, or self-destructive behaviors.

Spiritually, the absence of a father deprives a son of one of his most essential guides in understanding what it means to live a godly life. Fathers are meant to be the spiritual leaders of their homes, teaching their sons the importance of faith, prayer, and living according to biblical principles. When this is missing, the son may lack direction and spiritual grounding, making him more vulnerable to the lies and temptations presented by the Jezebel spirit. Jezebel thrives in environments where spiritual leadership is weak or absent, twisting the son's understanding of identity, purpose, and morality.

A father's absence also affects the son's relational development. Sons learn how to navigate relationships with God and others by observing their father's example. The son may struggle to form healthy, meaningful relationships when this example is missing or tainted. He may either become emotionally detached, fearing vulnerability and intimacy, or overcompensate by trying to control or dominate those around him, reflecting the manipulative patterns of the Jezebel spirit.

Additionally, the son may turn to unhealthy substitutes for the fatherly guidance he lacks. This could involve seeking validation in material success, dangerous behavior, or aligning himself with toxic male role models who perpetuate cycles of dysfunction and rebellion. The Jezebel spirit thrives in this atmosphere, promoting a false sense of masculinity based on control, domination, or indulgence rather than humility, strength, and service.

Ultimately, when a father fails to provide the emotional, spiritual, and moral foundation his son needs, it opens the door for the Jezebel spirit to infiltrate and disrupt the son's life. The absence of a strong, godly father figure can lead to broken identities, fractured relationships, and a skewed understanding of what it means to be a man of faith. Reclaiming this role is crucial, not only for the individual son's development but for breaking generational cycles of dysfunction and restoring God's intended order within the family.

For sons to thrive, they need the active presence of their father— someone who affirms their worth guides them spiritually, and models what it means to walk in godly character. When this foundation is in place, it equips sons to stand firm against the attacks of the Jezebel spirit and build their lives on the solid rock of faith, purpose, and identity in Christ.

Emotional Impact

Emotionally, sons without a present or engaged father often suffer from low self-esteem, identity confusion, and feelings of abandonment. The absence of a father figure leaves a gap that the Jezebel spirit will exploit, pressuring the son toward seeking validation in unhealthy relationships, gangs, or other harmful sources. Boys may grow up feeling unloved and unworthy, which makes them vulnerable to internalizing rejection. This emotional instability can lead to co-dependent or narcissistic behaviors later in life, as they continuously seek external validation that a father should have provided. They may also develop an unhealthy attachment with their mother, confusing them on properly growing and developing into a mature adult male.

Behavioral Impact

Behaviorally, a lack of fatherly leadership can result in rebellion and disrespect toward authority. The word of God states in Proverbs 22:6, *"Train up a child in the way he should go; even when he is old, he will not depart from it."* Without proper training and discipline from a father, a boy is more likely to fall into destructive behaviors, potentially crime, substance abuse, pornography, a fascination with death and destruction, and searching for a sense of belonging in the wrong places. Without a healthy example of godly masculinity, boys may adopt dysfunctional views of manhood, often manifesting as hyper-aggression or extreme passive irresponsibility.

Spiritual Impact

Spiritually, the absence of a father leaves boys exposed to Jezebel's narcissistic spiritual attack. From a Kingdom of Heaven standpoint, Fathers are charged with leading their household in the fear of the Lord

And these words, which I command thee this day, shall be in thine heart: and thou shalt teach them diligently unto thy children, and shalt talk of them when thou sittest in thine house, and when thou walkest by the way, and when thou liest down, and when thou risest up. And thou shalt bind them for a sign upon thine hand, and they shall be as frontlets between thine eyes. And thou shalt write them upon the posts of thy house, and on thy gates.- Deuteronomy 6:6-9

At the point when this is missing, the boy is often spiritually directionless, without the foundation to resist spiritual influences such as the Jezebel spirit, which thrives in confusion, chaos, and lack of direction. Ephesians 6:4 encourages fathers not to "*provoke their children to anger*" but to "*bring them up in the discipline and instruction of the Lord.*" When this is absent, boys may either fall into apathy or seek spiritual fulfillment in the occult, false religions, perversion, or secular ideologies.

Biblical Examples

Eli and His Sons - Eli, the high priest, neglected to properly discipline and train his sons in the ways of the Lord. As a result, his sons, Hophni and Phinehas, became corrupt and led the people astray, demonstrating how the absence of responsible fatherhood can lead to spiritual and moral decay.

Now the sons of Eli were worthless men. They did not know the Lord. The custom of the priests with the people was that when any man offered sacrifice, the priest's servant would come, while the meat was boiling, with a three-pronged fork in his hand, and he would thrust it into the pan or kettle or cauldron or pot. All that the fork brought up the priest would take for himself. This is what they did at Shiloh to all the Israelites who came there. Moreover, before the fat was burned, the priest's servant would come and say to the man who was sacrificing, "Give meat for the priest to roast, for he will not accept boiled meat from you but only raw." And if the man said to him, "Let them burn the fat first, and then take as much as you wish," he would say, "No, you must give it now, and if not, I will take it by

78

force." Thus the sin of the young men was very great in the sight of the Lord, for the men treated the offering of the Lord with contempt. - 1 Samuel 2:12-17

David and Absalom (read 2 Samuel 13-18) - David's failure to discipline his son Absalom after the rape of his sister Tamar resulted in Absalom's rebellion. This rebellion escalated into a full-scale attempt to overthrow his father David's kingdom. David's emotional disconnection with his son and failure to act as a responsible father led to his son's ruin and disorder in his family.

Isaac and Esau (read Genesis 25-27) - Isaac's preference toward Esau and his lack of spiritual teaching led to family dysfunction, disorder, strife, and deception that cost Esau his birthright and blessing. Esau's bitterness and separation from the family spiritually and emotionally emulates the modern effects of a father's failure to take responsibility and appropriate action.

In these examples, the cost of absent or negligent fatherhood is severe. Rebellion, spiritual degeneration, and destructive behavior all manifested. The Jezebel spirit seizes these moments of emotional and spiritual vulnerability, promoting a cycle of dysfunction and disorder that can perpetuate for generations. Fathers are expected to be protectors, teachers, givers, and spiritual leaders. When they fail in this role, the door is opened for Jezebel's bombardment of wicked attacks that leave much carnage within the family dynamics.

Wounded and Bitter Mothers

The Effect on Sons

When a mother or wife is abandoned by her husband, the emotional and psychological impact can be devastating. The pain, vulnerability, and sense of betrayal can leave deep wounds, and the Jezebel spirit quickly exploits these vulnerabilities. This spirit often manipulates the woman's role within the family, particularly affecting how she relates to her sons. One of the most destructive manifestations of the Jezebel spirit is its desire to control. In this case, it often operates by emasculating sons—stripping them of their masculine identity and authority, which can have lasting, far-reaching consequences on their development and future relationships.

The trauma of abandonment leaves many women feeling hurt, rejected, and insecure. The Jezebel spirit often takes advantage of these emotional wounds, manipulating the mother's brokenness into unhealthy patterns of control, fear, and mistrust. In an attempt to protect herself and her family from further pain or abandonment, the mother may feel compelled to assert control over her household. However, under Jezebel's influence, this desire for security can be twisted into a form of domination, especially over her sons, who now represent the male figures in the home.

As the mother grapples with her unresolved anger, disappointment, and pain, the Jezebel spirit may encourage her to project those emotions onto her sons. Subconsciously, she might view them through the lens of her husband's betrayal, treating them as though they are equally untrustworthy, inadequate, or likely to fail her. This dynamic can lead to controlling and overbearing behavior as the mother seeks to prevent her sons from making the same mistakes, she believes their father made.

This emasculation of sons has far-reaching consequences. Sons who grow up under the influence of a mother dominated by the Jezebel spirit may struggle with their sense of identity and masculinity. They may feel powerless or uncertain in their roles as men, having been stripped of their authority or confidence within the home. This dynamic can affect their relationships with others, making it difficult for them to assert themselves or develop healthy boundaries.

Over time, this control can also lead to strained relationships between the mother and her sons. The boys may feel suffocated by their mother's need to control every aspect of their lives, leading to rebellion, resentment, or emotional withdrawal. In extreme cases, they may either struggle to assert their own masculine identity or, conversely, develop an unhealthy pattern of seeking validation through dominance and control in their relationships—perpetuating the cycle of dysfunction that the Jezebel spirit thrives on.

Healing from this dynamic requires addressing the mother's emotional wounds and recognizing and breaking the influence of the Jezebel spirit. The mother must find healing in Christ, releasing the need to control and trusting God to provide the security and stability she seeks. By surrendering her pain and fear, she can begin to nurture her sons in a healthy way, allowing them to grow into confident, godly men, free from the manipulative grip of Jezebel's influence. For the sons, reclaiming their identity and authority in Christ will help them break free from the emasculating effects of control and grow into their God-given roles as strong, faithful leaders in their families and communities.

Emasculating the Sons: How the Jezebel Spirit Destroys Young Men

In a world where young men are increasingly disconnected from their genuine identity (in Christ) and purpose, the Jezebel spirit works subtly yet powerfully to emasculate sons and dismantle their God-given roles. This spirit seeks to undermine their strength, distort their sense of masculinity, and lure them into cycles of confusion, rebellion, and self-destruction. By attacking their confidence, honor, and spiritual foundation, Jezebel aims to weaken the next generation of men, rendering them ineffective and powerless as leaders, protectors, and godly influences. Let's investigate some of the methods Jezebel uses to emasculate sons and the destructive impact on young men.

Overprotection and Smothering

After being abandoned, a mother may become overly protective of her sons, seeking to shelter them from the difficulties she has endured. While protection is a natural instinct for a mother, the Jezebel spirit can take this to an extreme by cultivating an unhealthy emotional dependence between mother and son.

Lack of Independence

The mother may prevent or hinder her sons from developing independence, seeking instead to keep her sons dependent on her to maintain control over the son. The Jezebelic mother may shut down the decision-making abilities of the son and destroy any confidence the son may have that he can emancipate himself from "mommy." By doing so, she emasculates her sons, making them overly reliant on her for approval and direction.

Helicopter Parenting

The spirit might cause her to control every aspect of her sons' lives, from their relationships to their careers, their finances, and activities, never allowing them the opportunity to grow into their God-given masculine identity. This limits their ability to become strong, responsible, and capable men who can lead their own families in the future.

Undermining Masculine Authority

In some cases, the Jezebel spirit manipulates a mother's unresolved pain, causing her to develop a deep-seated resentment toward male authority as a whole. This bitterness often stems from past wounds, such as abandonment by her husband, neglect or abuse from her father, or painful experiences in previous relationships with men. These unhealed emotional scars create fertile ground for Jezebel to take root, twisting the mother's perception of male figures and authority.

As a result, this resentment can be subtly—or at times overtly—projected onto her sons, making it difficult for them to step into their God-given roles as men. Rather than supporting and encouraging their development into confident, strong leaders, the mother may sometimes undermine or stifle their growth without realizing it. This can manifest in various ways, from being overly critical or dismissive of their ambitions and decisions to controlling their actions to prevent them from exercising authority and responsibility.

The Jezebel spirit often distorts the mother's view of her sons, seeing them not as individuals with their own God-given identity but as potential threats or reminders of past pain. Instead of nurturing their masculine identity, she may unconsciously associate their growth into men with the same negative traits she experienced from other men in her life. This can lead to an emotional dynamic where the sons are either overly criticized, controlled or even infantilized—kept dependent and incapable of developing the strength and leadership qualities God intended for them.

The effects of this dynamic are profound. Sons growing up under this influence may feel disempowered, uncertain of their authority, or unable to confidently step into the male role that God has designed for them. They may internalize their mother's resentment toward male authority, leading them to question their masculinity or view it through a distorted lens. This can result in confusion, insecurity, or reluctance to embrace leadership in their families, churches, and communities later in life.

The mother's resentment toward male authority can also damage the mother-son relationship. The sons may feel suffocated, resentful, or misunderstood, sensing they are being held back from becoming the men they are meant to become. This dynamic can sometimes lead to rebellion, emotional withdrawal, or a strained, distant relationship with the mother. Over time, this continual undermining of their authority may cause the sons to retreat from responsibility or overcompensate, trying to assert dominance in unhealthy or destructive ways, perpetuating cycles of dysfunction.

Breaking this pattern requires deep emotional and spiritual healing for the mother. She must first acknowledge the unhealed wounds and resentment she harbors toward male authority and seek God's restoration and forgiveness. By releasing the pain and bitterness from past relationships and learning to trust God's design for her sons, she can allow them the freedom to grow into their roles as strong, godly men.

For the sons, reclaiming their identity and confidence as men of God is equally essential. They must learn to separate themselves from the emotional baggage projected onto them and embrace their God-given authority and role. With God's grace, the influence of the Jezebel spirit can be broken, enabling the mother to support her sons in healthy ways and allowing the sons to flourish into the men they were created to be—strong, faithful, and grounded in their purpose.

Criticism and Belittling

The mother may constantly criticize or belittle her sons out of frustration or an unconscious desire to prevent them from becoming like their father or to keep the son in submission to the controlling mother. This continuous undermining of their self-worth, value, and abilities as men can strip them of confidence, often leading to feelings of inadequacy, inferiority, and low self-esteem.

Questioning Their Leadership

As the sons grow older into adulthood, they may try to take on leadership roles in the home or a professional career, but the mother—operating under the influence of the Jezebel spirit—may resist this by questioning or rejecting their decisions, further emasculating them and reinforcing their sense of inferiority.

Emotional Manipulation

The Jezebel spirit thrives on manipulation, and in the context of a mother-son relationship, this can manifest as emotional control and demonic dominance. The mother might use guilt, shame, blame, condemnation, emotional withdrawal, and isolation to keep her sons in submission to her needs, preventing them from developing emotional intelligence, strength, and awareness.

Guilt and Obligation

The mother might make her sons feel guilty for pursuing their dreams or interests, using phrases like "After everything I've done for you" or "What will I do without you?" to create a sense of obligation. This keeps sons emotionally bound to their mother and prevents them from becoming independent, self-dependent males.

Emotional Dependency

A mother, driven by her emotional wounds and deficiencies, may unintentionally create an environment where her sons feel responsible for her emotional well-being. This dynamic is highly toxic and a clear sign that the Narcissistic-Jezebelic spirit is operating in full oppression mode. In such a dysfunctional setup, the sons are thrust into an unhealthy caregiving role, where they are expected to meet their mother's emotional needs.

This role reversal emasculates the sons by making them emotionally dependent on their mother rather than allowing them to grow into their God-given identity and strength. Instead of being nurtured and guided toward independence and spiritual leadership, they are burdened with the responsibility of managing their mother's emotional state. This undermines their development and distorts their understanding of healthy relationships. Rather than seeking their identity and strength in God, they become entangled in a codependent dynamic that stifles their growth as men.

This emotional burden causes the sons to lose sight of their purpose and authority in God, as they are constantly focused on appeasing or stabilizing their mother. Over time, this pattern erodes their confidence, self-worth, and ability to step into the masculine role they were designed for. It also fosters emotional confusion as they become entangled in a relationship that should be nurturing and supportive but instead is draining and disempowering.

Breaking free from this dynamic requires the mother and the sons to recognize the unhealthy pattern and seek healing. The mother must find emotional wholeness in God, releasing her sons from the burden of fulfilling needs only God can meet. The sons, in turn, must reclaim their independence and masculinity by anchoring their identity in God, freeing themselves from the Jezebelic control that has entangled them in an unhealthy emotional dependency.

Rejecting Male Role Models

One of the most damaging effects of the Jezebel spirit is the mother's potential rejection of positive male role models for her sons. Out of her pain and distrust of men, she may resist introducing or allowing strong, godly male figures to mentor her sons. She may speak harshly about men, calling them "dogs" or "useless." The Jezebel spirit designs this disparaging speech to see males as weak rather than the true leaders they are.

Blocking Godly Influence

If the mother's view of men is distorted by the abandonment, the Jezebel spirit may use this to block her sons from receiving guidance from male mentors like pastors, coaches, or family members. Without these positive male influences, the sons may struggle to develop their sense of manhood, leaving them spiritually and emotionally vulnerable. This may also cause the son to become effeminate, developing characteristics and behaviors generally associated with women.

Lack of Confidence

Sons emasculated by their mothers may grow up feeling unsure of their place in the world, unable to assert themselves or make decisions without feeling controlled or criticized. Often, they become prime targets for the spirit of Jezebel to manipulate and control, rendering the male ineffective in life.

Dysfunctional Relationships

Sons raised under the influence of a controlling Jezebelic mother often struggle in their relationships with women, either becoming overly passive or reacting by seeking control in unhealthy ways. This dynamic frequently leads to the development of narcissistic traits in men as they attempt to navigate the distorted family environment in which they were raised in. Their view of both femininity and masculinity becomes deeply skewed by Jezebel's influence, leading to an unhealthy understanding of gender roles.

As a result, these men may experience significant challenges in forming healthy, balanced relationships. Their passivity can make them susceptible to manipulation and control, while those who seek dominance may fall into patterns of emotional or relational abuse. The confusion between masculinity and femininity, ingrained through their dysfunctional upbringing, can lead to broken marriages, fractured families, and a cycle of relational dysfunction that is passed down to future generations.

The consequences of this Jezebelic influence reach far beyond individual relationships, contributing to a range of societal and generational problems. When men are unable to embrace their God-given roles with strength, integrity, and humility, it creates a ripple effect of dysfunction that impacts not only their personal lives but the well-being of their families and communities. Breaking this cycle requires a deep recalibration of identity—returning to God's design for healthy masculinity and femininity—and the breaking of generational strongholds that have distorted both.

Spiritual Passivity

Perhaps the most dangerous outcome is spiritual passivity. Without a solid masculine identity and an understanding of godly authority, these sons may become spiritually weak, failing to step into the roles God has for them as leaders and protectors.

When a mother operating under the influence of the Jezebel spirit exerts excessive control over her young son, it creates profound spiritual, emotional, and psychological issues. A controlling Jezebel mother often manipulates through emotional coercion, guilt, or fear, stifling the child's development and undermining his spiritual growth.

A Jezebel mother's control creates an atmosphere where the son may become spiritually apathetic or overly dependent on her instead of cultivating his relationship with God. This dependency can stifle spiritual growth, leaving the son spiritually immature and unprepared to take responsibility for his faith. The Jezebel spirit thrives on keeping the son from developing a solid spiritual life, which can result in a lack of discernment and an inability to resist temptation or external influences.

In the bible (2 Kings 8-9), Ahaziah was influenced by his mother, Athaliah, who was known for her control and wickedness. Under her control, Ahaziah followed in the ways of his mother's dysfunction, ultimately leading to his demise. This illustrates the danger of a controlling mother who operates under the influence of Jezebel and how it can lead sons away from the path of righteousness and toward spiritual decay.

The effect on daughters

It's essential to explore how the Jezebel spirit operates through wounded and bitter mothers to manipulate and distort their relationships with their daughters. The wounds of a bitter mother create fertile ground for the Jezebel spirit to sow seeds of dysfunction, which manifest in several toxic dynamics between mother and daughter. These dynamics not only cause emotional and psychological damage but also hinder the spiritual growth of the daughter, leaving her vulnerable to further attacks from the Jezebel spirit.

False Responsibility

One common tactic the Jezebel spirit uses is causing wounded mothers to place false responsibility on their daughters. In this scenario, the mother may treat the daughter as if she is responsible for her emotional well-being, marital problems, or even household responsibilities that are not appropriate for her age. The daughter is forced to carry the weight of adult burdens, known as "parentification." This false responsibility can severely limit the daughter's emotional development, as she is robbed of a proper childhood and forced into a caretaker role. The daughter may feel that her worth is tied to how well she performs these imposed responsibilities, leaving her prone to burnout, low self-esteem, and guilt when she inevitably falls short of her mother's unrealistic expectations. This emotional manipulation aligns with the Jezebel spirit's tactic of control and manipulation, as it keeps the daughter trapped in a cycle of striving for approval.

Competition Between Mother and Daughter

Another harmful dynamic the Jezebel spirit exploits is creating a sense of competition between mother and daughter. In this case, the wounded mother, out of her own insecurities, may see her daughter not as someone to nurture but as a rival. The mother may compete with the daughter over attention from others, including male figures like the daughter's father. She may criticize her daughter's appearance, talents, or personality, belittling her to maintain control and superiority. This can erode the daughter's sense of self-worth and confidence, making her feel inadequate and unloved. The spirit of Jezebel thrives in this environment of comparison, as it breeds jealousy, envy, and insecurity, pulling the daughter away from her God-given identity and purpose.

The competitive nature of such a relationship can also push the daughter to seek validation from external sources, such as unhealthy relationships, promiscuity, or attention-seeking behaviors, further exposing her to the Jezebel spirit's influence. Additionally, the competition may stunt the daughter's emotional development, as she is denied the nurturing love that a mother is meant to provide, instead being forced into a toxic, combative, and adversarial relationship.

The "Girlfriend" Dynamic

In some cases, the Jezebel spirit exploits the relationship by causing the mother to draw her daughter into an inappropriate "girlfriend" role. This dynamic occurs when the mother treats the daughter as a peer or confidante instead of acting as a parent and authority figure. The daughter becomes the mother's emotional sounding board, often being exposed to adult issues such as marital conflict, sexual details, or other personal struggles that are inappropriate for her to bear. In this dynamic, the mother may lean on the daughter for emotional support, violating the natural boundaries of the parent-child relationship. This places an undue emotional burden on the daughter, making her feel responsible for her mother's happiness or emotional stability.

This dysfunctional relationship often leaves the daughter feeling emotionally drained, confused, and disconnected from her own identity, as she is entangled in her mother's emotional world rather than focusing on her own development. The Jezebel spirit uses this dynamic to rob the daughter of the guidance, protection, and nurturing she needs from her mother. Furthermore, the lack of boundaries can create a sense of enmeshment, where the daughter struggles to establish her own identity separate from her mother, making her more susceptible to manipulation and control by others as she grows older.

Long-Term Impact

The long-term impact of these dysfunctional dynamics on the daughter's life is profound. Emotionally, she may grow up feeling burdened, inadequate, and resentful, constantly striving to meet the unrealistic expectations set by her mother. Psychologically, these dynamics can lead to anxiety, depression, and issues with self-worth, as the daughter is left feeling unloved and unsupported. Spiritually, the Jezebel spirit's influence disrupts the daughter's ability to form a healthy relationship with God. Her view of authority, love, and trust becomes skewed, often leading to a distorted perception of God's character and her identity in Christ.

Moreover, these dynamics may push the daughter into repeating the cycle in her future relationships, especially if the wounds inflicted by her mother go unhealed. Without spiritual intervention, the daughter may carry bitterness, resentment, or even a controlling spirit into her own family, perpetuating the influence of the Jezebel spirit across generations.

To protect daughters from the influence of the Jezebel spirit through wounded mothers, spiritual healing and deliverance are essential. Mothers must seek healing for their own wounds, allowing the Holy Spirit to break the chains of bitterness and hurt that make them vulnerable to Jezebel's manipulation. This healing process requires repentance, forgiveness, and the establishment of healthy emotional boundaries within the mother-daughter relationship. Daughters, too, need to be equipped with spiritual tools to break free from the false responsibility, competition, and unhealthy relational patterns instilled by the Jezebel spirit. By cultivating a strong sense of identity in Christ, daughters can reclaim their God-given purpose and avoid the traps laid by the Jezebel spirit.

Physical Abuse

The spirit of Jezebel uses physical abuse as a tool to influence a child's life by distorting their perception of love, security, and authority. Physical abuse creates an environment of fear and instability, where a child may grow up associating violence with normalcy. This leads to deep emotional and psychological wounds, making it easier for the spirit of Jezebel to manipulate the child's sense of identity and worth.

The trauma from physical abuse often results in feelings of rejection, unworthiness, and anger, leaving a child vulnerable to unhealthy coping mechanisms and a distorted view of relationships. It can also lead to cycles of self-destructive behavior, where the child either becomes abusive in their own relationships or remains in abusive situations, unable to break free. This vulnerability can lead the child to seek power or control in unhealthy ways, mimicking the manipulative and dominating characteristics associated with the Jezebel spirit.

Physical abuse can deeply fracture a child's spiritual foundations, especially when they experience consistent pain and suffering in a place where they should feel safe. As children develop, their understanding of love, trust, and authority is often linked to their family, particularly parental figures, who are meant to provide nurturing and protection. When those same figures become a source of harm, it can deeply damage the child's ability to grasp and experience the unconditional love of God.

Physical abuse can disconnect a child from their spiritual foundations, causing them to question God's love and protection, further isolating them from faith and opening the door for negative spiritual influences.

Doubt and Questioning God's Love and Protection

A child who endures physical abuse may wonder why God allows their suffering to occur, leading to confusion and doubt. They might ask, "If God loves me, why am I in pain?" or "Why doesn't God protect me from this harm?" These unanswered questions can cause a child to feel abandoned by God, creating emotional and spiritual distance. The child's understanding of love becomes associated with fear and punishment, making it difficult to believe in a loving, protective God.

Distorted Image of God

When the authority figures in a child's life—such as parents—are abusive, the child may project these characteristics onto their perception of God. If their experience of authority is harsh, punitive, or unloving, they may begin to see God in the same light, as a distant or even wrathful figure. This distorted image of God can push the child further away from seeking comfort or refuge in their faith, leaving them spiritually isolated.

Spiritual Disconnection

Over time, this growing disconnection from God can lead to spiritual emptiness, creating a void that the spirit of Jezebel seeks to fill. The child may become more vulnerable to negative spiritual influences as they search for power, control, or affirmation in unhealthy places. The Jezebel spirit can exploit this disillusionment by leading the child into rebellion against authority, manipulation, or unhealthy relationships—offering false empowerment and a counterfeit sense of belonging.

Isolation from other Believers

Children who experience abuse may also become isolated from supportive ministries and churches. They may feel unworthy or ashamed or reject faith altogether, believing that no one in the church understands their pain. This isolation can further weaken their spiritual defenses, making it easier for harmful influences to take root.

Addressing these spiritual wounds is critical for the child's healing journey. By restoring their trust in God's true nature—His love, mercy, and protection—the child can begin to rebuild their faith and reject the lies and manipulation of the Jezebel spirit.

What Is Physical Abuse?

Physical abuse is the intentional infliction of bodily harm or injury to another person. It involves using physical force in a way that causes pain, injury, or trauma to the victim. When it comes to children, physical abuse can occur in the home, at school, or in other environments where they should feel safe. This abuse often leaves physical and emotional scars, distorting the child's sense of safety, trust, and well-being.

Physical abuse is not limited to visible injuries; it also includes harmful physical actions that may not leave marks but still cause significant distress and harm.

Types of Physical Abuse

Hitting, Slapping, and Punching

This involves striking a child with hands, fists, or objects, causing bruising, cuts, and even internal injuries. Hitting or slapping can create a constant state of fear and confusion in the child, damaging their emotional and mental development.

Kicking

Kicking involves forcefully striking a child with the foot, often leading to severe bruising, broken bones, or internal injuries. This violent act can leave the child feeling powerless and vulnerable.

Burning

Inflicting burns using objects like cigarettes, irons, or hot liquids is another form of severe physical abuse. These burns can cause permanent physical disfigurement and psychological trauma.

Shaking

Shaking a child, especially an infant or toddler, can cause severe brain damage, known as *"shaken baby syndrome."* This can lead to lifelong cognitive disabilities, blindness, and even death.

Choking or Strangling

Choking or strangling involves restricting the child's ability to breathe, which can be terrifying and dangerous. This form of abuse often leaves the child traumatized, reinforcing a sense of helplessness.

Biting

Biting a child can cause puncture wounds, infections, and physical pain. It also sends a message of domination and control over the child's body, adding to the emotional trauma.

Throwing or Forcefully Handling

Throwing, dragging, or otherwise forcefully handling a child can result in severe physical injury, including broken bones or head trauma. Throwing objects such as dishes and other items is also considered physical abuse. These things can erode the child's sense of safety, leaving them in a constant state of anxiety and hyper-vigilance.

Pinching and Hair-Pulling

Though often considered less severe, pinching and hair-pulling are forms of physical abuse that cause pain, distress, and fear in the child. These acts reinforce a power imbalance and degrade the child's sense of worth.

Poisoning or Administering Harmful Substances

This includes giving a child harmful substances, such as drugs or alcohol, or using poison to harm them intentionally. These actions can result in severe health consequences and are a form of extreme physical abuse.

Withholding Necessary Medical Care

Failing to provide medical treatment for injuries or illnesses is also considered physical abuse. This neglect causes the child's health to deteriorate and shows a disregard for their well-being.

Emotional and Psychological Impact

Physical abuse doesn't just hurt the body; it also leaves deep emotional scars. The child often struggles with anxiety, depression, low self-esteem, and trust issues. Their relationship with authority and others can be severely impacted, leading them to isolate themselves or develop unhealthy patterns of behavior in an effort to regain control over their life.

Understanding these types of physical abuse helps in recognizing how the spirit of Jezebel might exploit such trauma to weaken a child's sense of worth, security, and connection to God.

Conclusion

The Jezebel spirit's attack on children is insidious and deeply destructive, targeting them at their most vulnerable stages of life. By exploiting emotional wounds, broken families, and distorted perceptions of authority and love, Jezebel weaves a web of deception that can lead children down paths of rebellion, confusion, and dysfunction. Whether through emotional manipulation, spiritual disconnection, or the erosion of their sense of identity, this spirit seeks to undermine their God-given potential and purpose.

However, understanding these tactics is the first step in breaking the cycle. As parents, leaders, and spiritual warriors, we must remain vigilant in protecting the hearts and minds of the next generation. By fostering environments rooted in God's truth, love, and affirmation, we can help shield children from Jezebel's influence and equip them with the tools to resist its grip. Through prayer, teaching, and intentional guidance, we can restore their sense of worth and identity in Christ, ensuring they grow into the confident, secure, and purpose-driven individuals God created them to be.

Our children are the future, and the battle for their hearts and minds is one we cannot afford to lose. With God's wisdom and guidance, we can stand firm against Jezebel's attacks and raise a generation equipped to fulfill their divine destiny, free from the chains of deception and spiritual bondage.

Chapter Three
Jezebel's Present-Day Influence on Youth

In the heart of modern society, an unseen battle rages for the souls of our youth. From social media to entertainment, education to family life, a subtle yet widespread force influences their thoughts, behaviors, identities, and faith. This force, rooted in the ancient character known as Jezebel, manifests today as a terrorist spirit that seeks to corrupt, manipulate, and control the younger generation. In the digital age, where culture often glorifies rebellion, vanity, and moral relativism, the Jezebel spirit subtly disguises and embeds itself in the various sectors of society and the institutions intended to nurture and guide children. As technology expands its reach and biblical values are increasingly attacked and destroyed, the Jezebel spirit finds new and innovative ways to infiltrate the minds and hearts of the youth, distorting their worldview, self-worth, and identity. In this chapter, we'll explore the multidimensional ways the Jezebel spirit manifests in society today, systematically targeting the most vulnerable—our children—through media, entertainment, education, and the family. By exposing these tactics, we can begin to understand how to educate, empower, protect, and deliver the next generation from its insidious grip.

- **Manipulation through Social Media and Pop Culture**

Social media has become a powerful tool for self-expression and connectivity, but it has also become a breeding ground for manipulation and deception. These platforms play a significant role in advancing the influence of the Jezebel spirit by promoting vanity, comparison, and superficiality. Through the constant barrage of curated content, youth are subtly drawn into a culture where external validation, self-promotion, and outward appearances are prioritized over inner character and spiritual growth.

The Jezebel spirit capitalizes on this dynamic, using social media and celebrity culture to manipulate young minds. Influencers often embody narcissistic traits like obsession with self, self-gratification, and dominance, creating an environment that glorifies these behaviors. As a result, youth are lured into adopting these values, fostering a self-centered worldview that undermines godliness and spiritual integrity. This constant focus on likes, followers, and external validation shifts their attention away from developing inner strength, humility, and a relationship with God.

Promotion of Vanity

Vanity is not merely a character flaw; it is a spiritual issue rooted in demonic influence, particularly the Jezebel spirit. At its core, vanity represents a form of self-worship, where an individual becomes fixated on their own appearance, achievements, and external validation. The Bible condemns such self-idolatry.

"The lofty looks of man shall be humbled, and the haughtiness of men shall be bowed down, and the Lord alone shall be exalted in that day" - Isaiah 2:11

Vanity plays a pivotal role in the manifestation of the Jezebel spirit because it shifts a person's focus entirely toward outward appearances and superficial gains, diverting them from God's purpose, identity, and truths. Under the influence of the Jezebel spirit, vanity becomes a pathway to self-idolatry, where individuals place themselves in the position of God, constantly seeking praise, attention, and admiration. This is a core strategy of the Jezebel spirit—luring individuals into forms of idolatry, making them more concerned with how they are perceived by others rather than how God sees them.

Moreover, the Jezebel spirit exploits vanity to create false identities. Encouraging individuals to obsess over their outward image distracts them from their true spiritual identity in Christ. Social media platforms such as Instagram, TikTok, and Snapchat amplify this dynamic, promoting image over substance. Youth are pressured to present idealized versions of themselves, driven by likes, followers, and views, perpetuating a culture of vanity where self-worth is tied to external validation. The Jezebel spirit thrives in this environment, fostering an excessive focus on appearance, status, and materialism. The fixation on self-glorification not only distracts youth from spiritual growth but also draws them deeper into a superficial lifestyle disconnected from God's truths.

These platforms are saturated with images and content that elevate wealth, beauty, and status, promoting narcissism as users strive to present an unrealistic, perfected version of themselves. This feeds into the Jezebel spirit's agenda, encouraging the belief that one's value is determined by outward appearance and social standing. As youth chase after validation based on appearance and material possessions, they become more susceptible to the Jezebel spirit's influence, which drives them to create a facade of perfection and hide their true selves.

The Jezebel spirit flourishes in this atmosphere, steering individuals to prioritize shallow qualities and external validation over inner growth, spiritual values, and genuine character. Self-obsession— one of the hallmarks of the Jezebel spirit—pulls young people away from their true spiritual purpose, leaving them vulnerable to deeper demonic influences.

The relentless pressure to appear perfect feeds directly into the Jezebel spirit's agenda of fostering pride, self-centeredness, and insecurity. Youth are vulnerable to this manipulation as they navigate the complexities of identity formation and seek approval from their peers. Social media, therefore, becomes a breeding ground for insecurity, shallow relationships, and self-obsession, playing right into the Jezebel spirit's hands by distracting youth from deeper, more meaningful pursuits. In this way, the spirit ensnares the hearts and minds of the younger generation, leading them further away from God and their true spiritual calling.

Comparing and Competing

We do not dare to classify or compare ourselves with some who commend themselves. When they measure themselves by themselves and compare themselves with themselves, they are not wise - 2 Corinthians 10:12

One of the most damaging aspects of social media is the comparison it fosters. Users constantly compare their lives, appearances, and successes with those they see online.

By constantly exposing youth to idealized versions of other people's lives, the spirit of Jezebel manipulates them into feeling inadequate or "less than." This leads to a toxic cycle of comparison. This comparison often involves unrealistic depictions of life, which create feelings of inadequacy, jealousy, and dissatisfaction. The Jezebel spirit takes advantage of this by sowing seeds of envy, rivalry, and resentment, encouraging a toxic mindset that focuses on what one lacks rather than being content or grateful. The Jezebel spirit uses comparison to erode self-esteem, causing young people to feel they are never good enough triggering emotional and psychological distress. As youth lose touch with their God-given identity, they become more vulnerable to external influences, seeking validation from worldly sources rather than divine truth.

Youth who engage in this cycle of comparison may feel compelled to outdo one another, becoming more competitive and self-absorbed in the process. This behavior leads to feelings of alienation, as their value becomes tied to how they measure up against others. The Jezebel spirit thrives in this environment, driving individuals away from humility and empathy while reinforcing a culture of self-promotion and competitiveness.

Perfect Lifestyles and Feelings of Inadequacy

Social media feeds are filled with images of seemingly perfect lives, showcasing wealth, beauty, success, and happiness. However, these lifestyles are often highly curated filtered, and do not reflect the reality behind the screen. The constant exposure to these unrealistic portrayals can cause young users to feel inadequate, as they believe they are falling short in comparison.

The Jezebel spirit uses fear and shame to control young people, making them feel inadequate or fearful of rejection if they do not conform to societal standards of beauty, success, or popularity.

Dysfunctional family dynamics, where abusive or manipulative authority figures control children, often mirror Jezebel's toxic influence. This can stifle emotional and spiritual development, leaving adolescents vulnerable to further spiritual oppression.

Spirit of Perfectionism

But he said to me, 'My grace is sufficient for you, for my power is made perfect in weakness.' Therefore I will boast all the more gladly about my weaknesses, so that Christ's power may rest on me. That is why, for Christ's sake, I delight in weaknesses, in insults, in hardships, in persecutions, in difficulties. For when I am weak, then I am strong - 2 Corinthians 12:9-10

The spirit of Jezebel preys on dissatisfaction, gradually eroding a young person's self-worth and confidence, leaving them vulnerable to deep emotional and spiritual wounds. As youth are lured into the relentless pursuit of perfection and validation from the world, they become disconnected from their true identity in Christ. This creates a cycle of anxiety, depression, and emptiness as they strive for unattainable ideals set by society, often forgetting the inherent value and worth that God has placed within them.

Desperate to meet these impossible standards, they lose sight of their divine purpose, becoming trapped in a perpetual state of self-doubt and insecurity. The Jezebel spirit thrives in this environment, using the constant chase for worldly affirmation to push them further away from God's truth. Instead of resting in the knowledge that they are fearfully and wonderfully made, young people are left emotionally unstable, spiritually disconnected, and vulnerable to deeper demonic influences.

By making youth believe that their worth is tied to external success, appearance, or societal approval, the Jezebel spirit keeps them locked in a state of spiritual bondage. This manipulation causes them to prioritize worldly standards over God's calling, resulting in a life consumed by comparison, perfectionism, and an insatiable need for validation. Ultimately, the spirit's mission is to keep them from discovering the peace, joy, and purpose that come from embracing their true identity in Christ.

Impact on Self-Worth and Identity

Social media's influence can severely impact how young people perceive themselves, as their self-worth becomes tied to the number of likes, followers, or comments they receive. Low self-worth often leads youth to adopt false identities, trying to mimic influencers or celebrities. This opens them to greater spiritual vulnerability as they move further away from their true identity in Christ, falling prey to a destructive cycle of comparison, insecurity, and dissatisfaction. The Jezebel spirit manipulates this, making youth increasingly dependent on external validation for their sense of value instead of drawing their worth from within or their relationship with God. This can lead to identity confusion, low self-esteem, and a constant need for approval, which further distances them from their true purpose and calling.

Music

Certain types of music today actively glorify behaviors and attitudes that resonate with the Jezebel spirit's influence, promoting rebellion against authority, sexual promiscuity, substance abuse, and even the demonic. These themes, commonly found in genres like modern hip-hop, rock, and electronic music, are not merely entertainment but serve as subtle yet powerful tools of influence, particularly for impressionable young minds.

Lyrics that glamorize violence, for example, can desensitize listeners to the seriousness of such actions, leading to a hardened heart that struggles to discern right from wrong. This parallels how the spirit of Jezebel, as depicted in the Bible, seduced and manipulated others to draw them away from God's truth, gradually weakening their moral compass.

In addition, many songs today celebrate sexual exploitation and corruption, distorting how youth perceive relationships, morality, and societal norms. When songs repeatedly promote aggression or objectify women, they condition young listeners to view love and respect through a skewed, dehumanizing lens. Over time, this can result in a desensitization to the values of empathy, respect, and self-worth, undermining the spiritual and moral foundation essential for a healthy life.

Similarly, music that glorifies substance abuse or even dabbles in occult themes normalizes these destructive behaviors, encouraging experimentation and rebellion against traditional moral frameworks. By continually consuming music with these messages, youth may question the importance of values such as purity, obedience, and self-discipline—cornerstones of spiritual growth and maturity.

Songs that promote hopelessness, despair, and negativity plant dangerous seeds of emotional and spiritual turmoil in young minds. Likewise, lyrics that incite violence, hatred, racism, or disrespect for authority figures like teachers and law enforcement feed into the Jezebel spirit's agenda of moral decay. These toxic messages contribute to a path of destruction, fostering emotional instability, rebellion, and a disconnect from God's truth.

As young people internalize the harmful messages found in certain music, it often manifests in behavioral problems, addiction, and a general disrespect for both moral and spiritual authority. Their hearts become hardened towards others and God Himself, further highlighting the critical need for discernment in the media and music consumed today. Parents and guardians must guide their children in making wise choices about the music they listen to, ensuring it aligns with values that promote spiritual growth, emotional well-being, and godly character.

Perversion of Identity and Sexuality

At the core of the Jezebel spirit's manipulation through social media and pop culture is a direct assault on the identity of young people. Just as Jezebel promoted sexual immorality in ancient Israel, this spirit continues to corrupt the understanding of identity and sexuality in today's youth.

Modern media, entertainment, and even educational systems often promote confusing and ungodly perspectives on gender, sexuality, and relationships, pulling young people away from biblical truth. The Jezebel spirit thrives in environments of confusion, instability, and insecurity—precisely the atmosphere that social media and pop culture cultivate. Adolescents are bombarded with messages that glorify promiscuity, sexual experimentation, and distorted views of love and identity, leading to dysfunction in their understanding of what healthy relationships should be.

Social media platforms, in particular, encourage the creation of multiple personas—one for the preferred online presence and another for real life. This duality leads to deep confusion about who they truly are. The Jezebel spirit seizes upon this confusion, enticing young people to adopt false identities, often rooted in sexual expression or conformity to societal pressures. As they conform to peer groups and cultural trends, they drift further from their God-given identity and purpose.

This identity crisis among today's youth has created a spiritual void—a vacuum that the Jezebel spirit is quick to fill with destructive and toxic influences. By undermining the biblical foundation of identity and replacing it with distorted views of self-worth and relationships, this spirit perpetuates emotional instability, insecurity, and spiritual disconnection, leaving youth vulnerable to further deception and bondage.

Hyper-Sexualization – The Destruction of Innocence

One of the most insidious tactics of the Jezebel spirit is the promotion of hyper-sexualization, which leads to the erosion of innocence in today's youth. Many social media platforms glorify hyper-sexualized content, encouraging young people to explore and exploit their sexuality at a dangerously early age. The Jezebel spirit works through these platforms, such as TikTok and Instagram, to desensitize youth to godly standards of purity and morality. Through sexually suggestive dances, provocative imagery, and influencers who equate sexual attention with validation and power, young minds are subtly manipulated into believing that their self-worth is tied to their ability to attract and maintain sexual attention.

This bombardment of hyper-sexualized content leads to the moral degradation of young people, placing them on a destructive path toward spiritual corruption, where they become bound by lust and promiscuity. The Jezebel spirit's goal is to distort God's original design for healthy relationships and sexuality, replacing it with a counterfeit version that leads to profound emotional and spiritual harm. This manipulation creates a breeding ground for demonic sexual soul ties, emotional fragmentation, and confusion about their true identity and worth in Christ.

As young people embrace these behaviors, many experience the weight of guilt, shame, and a loss of self-respect, which further drives them into demonic oppression. They become entangled in a cycle of promiscuity and lust, where they seek validation through sexual exploitation but are left empty and broken inside. This emotional and spiritual emptiness deepens the hold of the Jezebel spirit, making it harder for them to break free and return to a place of godly purity and spiritual wholeness.

Finally, in the information age, social media has become a double-edged sword. While it has the potential to empower and connect, it can also be a tool of destruction if used indiscriminately. Parents must teach and train their children to navigate these platforms with discernment, helping them understand the dangerous outcomes of following the patterns of the world. Social media and pop culture have become potent weapons in the hands of the Jezebel spirit, meticulously designed to lure young people into emotional, spiritual, and moral bondage.

By promoting vanity, comparison, hyper-sexualization, rebellion, and materialism, the Jezebel spirit systematically dismantles the spiritual integrity of youth, leading them into cycles of destruction, confusion, and demonic oppression. The reality is that many young people are being drawn away from God's truth and led down a path of spiritual ruin. Awareness of these tactics is crucial in combating the spiritual forces at play. It is our responsibility to guide youth back to their true identity in Christ, helping them reclaim their innocence and equipping them to stand firm in purity, truth, and freedom amid a corrupt, dark culture.

- **Entertainment**

The Jezebel spirit exploits the entertainment arena in numerous ways. From movies and television to fashion, video games, and even sports, these platforms serve as powerful vehicles to influence and attack the hearts and minds of youth. Through the glamorization of sin, the normalization of rebellion, and the distortion of moral values, the entertainment industry often perpetuates messages that align with the Jezebel spirit's agenda, subtly shaping the worldview of young people.

One of the key strategies the Jezebel spirit employs is turning celebrities into modern-day idols. In today's culture, youth often model their behavior, appearance, and values after the celebrities they admire. The Jezebel spirit encourages this idolatry, drawing young people to place their trust, admiration, and energy into following public figures rather than God. As they idolize these celebrities, they begin to turn away from godly role models, adopting behaviors and beliefs that can lead to spiritual and emotional destruction. This form of idolatry disconnects them from their true identity in Christ, pushing them toward shallow, superficial, and worldly pursuits.

The Jezebel spirit also leverages the entertainment arena to promote materialism, convincing youth that their worth is tied to what they own or the lifestyle they portray. This distortion of values drives them to focus on accumulating wealth and possessions rather than cultivating spiritual virtues like humility, generosity, and contentment. Many young people are mesmerized by the glamorous lifestyles of entertainers and sports figures, fixating on gold chains, luxury cars, and designer clothes. As a result, their sense of reality becomes distorted, and they lose sight of the importance of spiritual growth and godly character.

Through this manipulation of entertainment, the Jezebel spirit systematically draws young people away from their God-given purpose and into a life defined by superficial desires and worldly standards, creating spiritual and emotional instability.

Movies, Reality TV, and Normalization of Wickedness

The Jezebel spirit also uses film and television to normalize sin, distorting what is good and evil. TV shows and movies often depict immoral relationships, glorify promiscuity, celebrate substance abuse, and present rebellious characters as heroes. This subtle manipulation causes young people to view these behaviors as acceptable, even aspirational. By repeatedly seeing sinful behaviors glorified on screen, youth become desensitized to the moral consequences of their actions. They begin to justify sin, believing that what they see in pop culture is normal and desirable. Over time, this leads to spiritual blindness and emotional disillusionment.

Reality TV often promotes ungodly values such as vanity, competition, materialism, and manipulation, all traits closely aligned with the Jezebel spirit. These shows typically celebrate drama, deceit, and toxic relationships, glorifying self-centered and sensationalizing jealousy.

Reality TV personalities often become narcissistic-Jezebelic influencers, representing exaggerated lifestyles that thrive on attention, vanity, and superficial success. The Jezebel spirit operates through these influencers by promoting a culture of comparison, encouraging youth to emulate wicked behaviors. Vulnerable viewers may develop unrealistic expectations for their lives, becoming overly concerned with appearances, or internalize the selfish, manipulative behaviors displayed on these shows.

In many cases, the content encourages rebellion against authority and lustful and aggressive behaviors that display characters manipulating situations to gain an advantage over their peer rivals. Through repeated exposure, the Jezebel spirit uses these influences to create confusion around moral values, further disconnecting youth from their spiritual foundation.

Some popular shows that exhibit behaviors and values associated with the Jezebel spirit are:

Keeping Up with the Kardashians – This narcissistic show revolves around the Kardashian family and promotes excessive materialism, vanity, and superficiality. The constant focus on appearance, fame, and fortune reinforces values like self-indulgence and the pursuit of external validation, all characteristic of the Jezebel spirit. Much of the show focuses on celebrity culture, family drama and conflict, romantic relationships, and sexuality. The Kardashians' romantic relationships, breakups, and personal scandals are central to the show, often involving highly publicized romantic entanglements, marriages, and divorces. The content frequently pushes themes of sexual freedom and romantic deception.

These features, which center on vanity, materialism, and drama, reflect many aspects of the Jezebel spirit, promoting values inconsistent with the Christian faith and hindering spiritual growth and development.

The Real Housewives franchise – This venomous series often portrays drama, gossip, manipulation, and competition among wealthy women. The focus on conflict, rivalry, and selfish ambition aligns with the

Jezebel spirit's traits of divisiveness and control, encouraging viewers to normalize toxic relationships and behavior.

Love Island – A diabolical reality dating show where contestants compete for love and money. This show emphasizes sexual promiscuity, lust, and manipulation, with contestants using their charm and appearance to gain the upper hand, which parallels the Jezebel spirit's tactics of seduction and emotional control.

These shows promote ideals contrary to biblical teachings, reinforcing the Jezebel spirit's influence on youth through their glamorous but ultimately dull and destructive portrayals of life.

Video games

In today's digital age, video games have become a central form of entertainment for youth, offering immersive experiences and an escape from reality and ushering them into a virtual world that many get lost within. Beneath the surface awaits the spirit of Jezebel, who uses this metaverse filled with avatars and augmented reality to infiltrate the minds and hearts of young people, leading them down the dark path of desensitization.

Through violent, hyper-sexualized, and addictive content, video games desensitize youth to aggression, normalize immoral behavior, and create a disconnect from reality and responsibility. By promoting rebellion, instant gratification, and escapism, the Jezebel spirit shrewdly gains control, hindering emotional, social, and spiritual development and making young people more vulnerable to Jezebel's arsenal of toxic tactics.

Violent video games immerse players in highly aggressive scenarios where violence is rewarded and normalized. Repeated exposure can desensitize young players to real-life violence, reducing empathy and emotional responses to aggression. Jezebel works hard to get our youth to view violent behavior as more acceptable or less severe. This leads to the increased likelihood of aggressive behavior, bullying, or even dramatic violent outbursts. The Jezebel spirit can use these games as a tool to erode moral boundaries, making destructive behavior seem commonplace ultimately leading to behavioral problems.

Additionally, video games, especially online ones, can be highly addictive due to their instant gratification, intensive, challenging features, and reward systems. The spirit of Jezebel capitalizes on this by building up a dependency on these games, pulling children away from interpersonal relationships, self-discipline, and spiritual growth. Through excessive gaming, children may become increasingly isolated, anxious, or even obsessed, diverting them from their true purpose in life and spiritual connection to God.

Obsessive video and online gaming lead to a steady detachment from reality, as children and teenagers alike become more absorbed in the virtual reality world. This detachment results in weakened family bonds and friendships, as the child's emotional and social development is stunted due to the lack of real-world interaction. Often, they struggle to communicate or engage in meaningful relationships outside of the game. The spirit of Jezebel seeks to isolate and control, making it harder for these children to build healthy connections or be accountable to those who genuinely love and care about them.

Video games can be a gateway for the Jezebel spirit to manipulate and control youth. Parents need to be aware of this demonic tributary used by Jezebel to bring children into bondage. Discuss with your child the importance of setting healthy boundaries and the potential dangers of excessive gaming, in addition to the demonic underworld strategy to destroy the next generation through the abuse of virtual and augmented reality platforms.

- **Education**

Secular Indoctrination

Since the founding of the United States, America's educational system has been deeply rooted in Christian principles and values. For centuries, schools reinforced biblical teachings, shaping students' moral framework. However, this began to change by the turn of the 19th century. By the 1960s, with the rapid rise of secular ideologies, the Supreme Court effectively removed Christian influence from public education. This shift paved the way for the erosion of moral and spiritual values in schools, leaving a void that secular teachings have eagerly filled.

The removal of Christian education from schools is a significant factor in the rise of secular ideologies, which often seek to replace God with Jezebelic-inspired principles. These teachings aim to undermine moral absolutes and biblical authority, fostering confusion and manipulation among young minds. Without a clear ethical framework grounded in God's Kingdom, children are left without the tools to discern right from wrong, making them more vulnerable to demonic oppression and the deceptive allure of moral relativism. The absence of scripture-based education strips away opportunities to understand absolute truth, divine authority, and God's original purpose for humanity. This allows the Jezebel spirit to thrive by promoting the idea that truth is subjective, and morality is fluid.

The Jezebel spirit capitalizes on this environment, using secular ideologies to draw young people away from biblical values. When students are not taught to stand on the firm foundation of God's truth, they may more easily adopt beliefs that oppose the Kingdom of God. For example, secular ideologies may normalize abortion (murder), casual sex (fornication), and a hedonistic mindset of 'if it feels good, do it' (lust of the flesh). In this framework, everyone's personal interpretation of truth is considered equally valid, creating fertile ground for the Jezebel spirit to operate through deception, eliminating established moral and spiritual values.

Secular ideologies that reject God's word normalize behaviors that were once seen as morally unacceptable. These include materialism, sexual openness, and the rejection of any form of restraint—all values that align with the Jezebel spirit's methods of manipulation and control. The Bible, particularly in Revelation, warns believers not to tolerate the teachings of Jezebel, yet today's secular educational system fosters the very principles she represents.

In many cases, the secular educational system emphasizes conformity over creativity and critical thinking, which directly conflicts with the values of the Kingdom of God. Youth are often pushed to conform to societal norms that promote materialism, individualism, and relativism, diminishing their spiritual discernment. Rather than fostering moral and spiritual development, the system subtly prioritizes academic success, career ambition, and social status over a relationship with God and adherence to biblical principles. The Jezebel spirit works tirelessly to draw the youth into the collective ideologies of a godless world system, undermining their spiritual growth.

Much of today's curricula leave little room for God, spiritual growth, or moral consideration, instead promoting ideologies that elevate the flesh and idolize humanity. This kind of indoctrination stifles individual thought, choice, and creativity, leading to a generation that lacks the courage to challenge the dominant culture. As a result, many young people grow up spiritually adrift, struggling with their identity, purpose, and the meaning of life. Without a spiritual foundation, they are left searching for answers in secular ideologies that are spiritually void. The Jezebel spirit exploits this void, filling it with rebellion, vanity, promiscuity, perversion, control, manipulation, and the glorification of self.

Ultimately, the removal of Christian education and the rise of secular ideologies are part of the Jezebel spirit's broader plan to lead youth away from God, distort their sense of identity, and trap them in a cycle of moral and spiritual confusion.

Erosion of Authority

The removal of Christian education from schools has eliminated biblical teaching and diminished the influence and acceptance of parental and institutional authority in moral instruction. As Christian values are stripped away, the Jezebel spirit seizes this opportunity to further erode respect for established authority structures, including the family, church, civil laws, and societal institutions. By undermining these foundational pillars, the Jezebel spirit encourages a culture of rebellion, where the guidance of parents, teachers, and spiritual leaders is no longer valued or heeded.

This deliberate erosion of Christian education and moral authority creates fertile ground for the Jezebel spirit to infiltrate youth culture. Without the anchoring presence of biblical truth and parental authority, many young people become vulnerable to ideologies that promote defiance, self-reliance, and a rejection of godly principles. The Jezebel spirit thrives in this atmosphere, fostering an attitude of rebellion against parental guidance and spiritual and societal laws designed to preserve moral order.

As the influence of Christian moral instruction fades, entire generations are left disconnected from God, with no clear moral compass to guide their decisions and actions. The result is a steady decline in spiritual awareness, where the values of obedience, respect, and submission to divine and earthly authority are replaced by a pursuit of individualism, self-gratification, and moral relativism. The Jezebel spirit uses this spiritual void to implant beliefs and behaviors that erode spiritual sensitivity and sever the connection between young people and their Creator.

This widespread rebellion against authority is seen in family dynamics and societal structures at large, as youth increasingly question and defy civil laws, church teachings, and the ethical frameworks that once held society together. The spirit of Jezebel actively works to replace respect for these systems with a mindset of pride, autonomy, and rejection of any authority that would call for accountability or submission to God's order. This, in turn, leads to a broader moral and ethical decline, as the very institutions that once safeguarded spiritual and moral integrity are sidelined, and secular ideologies take root.

Ultimately, by removing Christian and biblically based moral education from schools, society has opened the door for the Jezebel spirit to influence young minds. This spirit promotes a belief system that not only undermines spiritual awareness but also drives entire generations into deeper moral decay, disconnecting them from God's truth and leading them down a path of spiritual destruction.

Religious Systems

The Jezebel spirit is infamous for infiltrating religious institutions, churches, ministries, and networks through false teachings, manipulation, perversion, and corruption. It affects both leadership and congregations alike. This spirit often manifests through leaders who misuse their authority, promote doctrines that deviate from sound biblical teaching, or engage in self-serving behavior under the guise of spiritual guidance. This manipulation fosters an environment of control and oppression within the church, stifling genuine spiritual growth and leading to mass spiritual destruction among the flock.

Within churches and ministries, the Jezebel spirit works through teachings catering more to worldly desires than biblical righteousness. Today, many youth are exposed to compromised leaders who engage in scandals, inappropriate relationships, and corruption. Some churches have watered down the Gospel message, transforming gatherings into entertainment hubs rather than equipping centers for spiritual warfare and discipleship. This confusion leaves youth spiritually disoriented, unaware of the authority they have in Christ to combat the Jezebel spirit's attacks.

A lack of genuine, Kingdom-minded leaders, teachers, mentors, and coaches only amplifies this issue. Without strong, biblically grounded leaders, young people often feel disconnected from their faith, leading to apathy or disillusionment. When they don't experience authentic discipleship or witness integrity in leadership, they may be tempted to turn away from God or fall prey to secular ideologies. The Jezebel spirit thrives in this environment, sowing seeds of doubt and confusion, ultimately undermining the spiritual foundation that youth desperately need.

This spirit often infiltrates leadership, seeking fame, power, money, or personal gain rather than serving God and the people they are called to lead. These leaders may preach messages that twist Scripture to justify immoral behavior or worldly success, distorting the true essence of the Gospel. For example, teachings that promote prosperity over humility, personal ambition over servanthood, or the desires of the flesh over the leading of the Holy Spirit are clear indicators of this deception.

The Jezebel spirit's influence is subtle yet pervasive. It often manifests as a spiritual authority within the church, controlling the narrative, silencing dissent, and manipulating followers to align with the leader's fleshly desires rather than God's will. This creates an environment where questioning or seeking deeper biblical understanding is discouraged, leading to spiritual stagnation and dependence on defective leadership. The Jezebel spirit will frequently misuse spiritual language, claiming to speak on behalf of God with phrases like "God told me," while in reality, they are operating under a false authority driven by Jezebel's influence.

Corruption within churches and ministries influenced by the Jezebel spirit takes many forms: financial mismanagement, immoral conduct, or aligning the church with secular ideologies for the sake of cultural relevance. It may also manifest through nepotism, favoritism, or using the pulpit to advance personal agendas, political biases, and secular activism. These actions erode the integrity of the ministry and breed confusion, especially among younger members who seek authenticity in their relationship with God. When youth encounter leaders who live contrary to the teachings they preach, it breeds mistrust, leaving a void that the Jezebel spirit can further exploit through false comfort in secular ideologies or entice them toward rebellion and apathy.

Without genuine discipleship, young people may feel spiritually orphaned. When churches prioritize performance, entertainment, or outward appearances rather than nurturing a deep relationship with Christ, youth become disengaged from the Word of God and more attracted to superficial distractions. They are left vulnerable to ideologies that promise empowerment, freedom, or self-fulfillment but ultimately lead them away from God.

The Jezebel spirit also operates subtly within the general congregation. It sows discord through gossip, slander, and backbiting among members, leading to fractured relationships, cliques, and factions that disrupt the peace and unity of the church. Those influenced by Jezebel spread rumors, harshly criticize others, and focus on faults, all of which damage trust and undermine the faith community. Additionally, Jezebel stirs up a spirit of competition within the church, encouraging an unhealthy focus on titles, positions, and status. Vanity and pride take root as members become more concerned with appearances and social standing than spiritual integrity.

Another subtle but powerful influence of the Jezebel spirit is fostering complacency in the spiritual walk. Those affected may lose their hunger for the Word, neglect prayer, and become lukewarm in their faith. They may attend church services out of obligation but remain disengaged from true worship, deliverance, and spiritual warfare, leaving them vulnerable to further attacks.

Furthermore, the Jezebel spirit distorts believers' view of authority. Even when there are no genuine issues with leadership, those caught in Jezebel's web may harbor resentment or distrust towards spiritual authority, questioning teachings and promoting rebellion. This leads to a subtle undermining of the authority of Scripture and the leaders who uphold it.

Rather than encouraging a heart of service and humility, the Jezebel spirit fosters self-centeredness. Church members may seek recognition or personal gain through their service, turning worship into a performance rather than a sincere offering to God. This focus on self erodes the sense of community and mutual edification that should define Christian fellowship.

Additionally, the Jezebel spirit lures young believers to compromise their faith with worldly values, a major tactic today. It begins by promoting tolerance for sin, convincing individuals that behaviors such as sexual immorality, materialism, or moral relativism are acceptable. This compromise weakens the body of Christ, rendering it less effective in being a transformative influence in the world.

The Jezebel spirit often manipulates through emotional instability, playing on feelings of rejection, loneliness, or fear. Those affected may become easily offended, highly reactive, or prone to emotional manipulation, creating instability and division within the body of Christ.

Today, many churches, leaders, and believers have fallen prey to the Jezebel spirit, whether through scandal, moral decay, or the suppression of truth. The absence of sound doctrine, accountability, and a servant's heart creates fertile ground for the Jezebel spirit to flourish, turning houses of worship into places of control, manipulation, and deception.

The Occult

Attraction to the Occult

In today's world, occult practices are intricately woven into popular culture through social media, music, television shows, fashion, advertising, and even personal growth ideologies. Astrology apps, zodiac memes, and Eastern mysticism are marketed as fun and harmless, subtly conditioning young minds to seek guidance from cosmic alignments or fortune tellers instead of turning to God. Witchcraft and sorcery are often glamorized as forms of empowerment, especially for those who feel powerless or oppressed, offering the illusion of control through spells, rituals, and other esoteric practices.

The Jezebel spirit skillfully exploits this cultural shift, presenting the occult as a path to self-discovery and empowerment. In their search for identity, meaning, and purpose, youth are particularly vulnerable to this deception. Without a solid spiritual foundation, they may be drawn to the mysticism of the occult, which promises quick answers, personal empowerment, and spiritual enlightenment—concepts that seem attractive in a secular, materialistic world. New Age philosophies, which often claim to be inclusive and non-religious, further appeal to youth by offering a seemingly non-judgmental alternative to traditional Christianity. These philosophies frequently include ideas such as 'manifesting your reality' or 'channeling energy,' which entice young people seeking control over their circumstances or a sense of power over themselves. The Jezebel spirit uses these practices to draw youth into deception, pulling them away from God and sound biblical doctrine.

Once youth engage in these practices, the spiritual dangers become increasingly severe. Occult involvement opens a direct doorway to demonic forces operating in the unseen realm. Whether through astrology, tarot cards, crystals, or witchcraft rituals, young people unknowingly invite demonic influences that aim to enslave, deceive, and ultimately destroy. This interaction can result in demonic oppression or even possession, manifesting in various ways, such as spiritual blindness, night terrors, phobias, depression, anxiety, and even physical ailments.

The psychological and emotional toll of engaging in the occult is profound. Youth immersed in these practices often experience deep isolation as they drift further from relationships with family, friends, and God. They may also battle fear and confusion as the demonic forces behind these practices manipulate their thoughts and emotions, leading to mental instability. What initially appears to be an empowering journey often leaves them feeling hopeless and empty, as the promised power and fulfillment never materialize.

The bondage that accompanies occult involvement is not only psychological but deeply spiritual. Youth trapped in these practices may find themselves caught in cycles of obsession or addiction, constantly seeking more knowledge or power but never finding peace. The Jezebel spirit thrives on this deception, keeping individuals bound and preventing them from experiencing true freedom in Christ. In more severe cases, this spiritual bondage may compel individuals to delve into darker forms of occultism, further increasing their vulnerability to demonic attacks.

As youth become more comfortable with occult practices, they grow desensitized to the reality of spiritual warfare and deliverance. What begins as innocent curiosity can quickly spiral into deeper involvement as they become increasingly familiar with these dark spiritual practices. Engaging in the occult aligns with the Jezebel spirit's witchcraft and opens doors to demonic oppression. Youth who participate in occult activities may unknowingly enter into spiritual covenants with dark forces, leading to severe spiritual bondage. The Jezebel spirit deceives them into believing they are gaining control or insight, but in reality, they are granting demonic forces legal authority to torment and enslave them.

The deeper youth engage with these practices, the more they align themselves with spiritual forces opposed to God's Kingdom, drawing them further from biblical truth. Ultimately, the Jezebel spirit uses these deceptive practices to lead youth into spiritual darkness, blinding them to the light of God's truth and the freedom found in Christ.

Families

The Jezebel spirit cultivates family dysfunction, primarily by undermining parental authority and sowing seeds of rebellion in children. This spirit encourages youth to reject the wisdom and guidance of their parents and biblical principles in favor of independence, self-rule, and self-gratification—values that align with the Jezebel spirit's inherent disdain for authority. By promoting these ideas, the Jezebel spirit leads young people to believe that defiance is a sign of strength and autonomy, subtly driving a wedge between parents and their children.

This spirit's influence often results in fractured family relationships, as children become resistant to correction and discipline, perceiving it as an infringement on their personal freedom. Parental guidance is seen as outdated or oppressive, leading to a breakdown of trust and communication. This erosion of respect for authority affects the immediate family and perpetuates generational cycles of rebellion, manipulation, and control—much like the legacy of Jezebel's influence, which extended to her descendants.

Furthermore, the Jezebel spirit exploits dysfunction within the family structure, whether it be through absent or abusive parents, broken relationships, or unresolved trauma. By sowing chaos and division, this spirit capitalizes on the emotional and spiritual void created by dysfunctional environments, leaving children vulnerable to manipulation and deception. Without a strong, godly foundation, young people are more likely to seek validation, acceptance, and power through unhealthy means, often mirroring the control and manipulation tactics embodied by the Jezebel spirit.

In this way, the Jezebel spirit not only distorts the child's view of authority but also perpetuates a cycle of dysfunction, ensuring that the wounds of one generation are passed on to the next. It weakens the family unit, which is meant to be a place of safety, guidance, and spiritual growth, and replaces it with confusion, conflict, and rebellion. Ultimately, the spirit of Jezebel seeks to sever the family's connection to God, replacing His divine order with chaos and strife and leading young people down a path of spiritual rebellion and emotional instability.

Family Dysfunction in the Bible

The Bible contains numerous accounts of family dysfunction that led to cycles of toxic behaviors and consequences for the offspring involved. Many of these stories highlight how unresolved family issues, traumas, generational sins, and toxic relationships can deeply impact children, often leading them astray from God's path. Here are just a few worth mentioning:

King David and His Family

David's family is one of the Bible's most well-known examples of family dysfunction. David's failure as a father to discipline his children, together with having multiple wives (women), led to heartbreaking consequences.

Amnon and Tamar - David's son, Amnon, had a spirit of lust and raped his half-sister, Tamar, leading to family disgrace and unresolved trauma. Again, David failed to take appropriate action against Amnon, causing a ripple effect of tension in his family (2 Samuel 13:1-22).

Absalom - Tamar's full brother, Absalom, took matters into his own hands by murdering Amnon in revenge. Later, Absalom turned against David, leading a rebellion to overthrow his father as king (2 Samuel 13:23-29; 15:1-14). This rebellion resulted in Absalom's death and intense grief for David (2 Samuel 18:33).

David's lack of leadership within his family led to dysfunctional relationships, strife, and disastrous outcomes for his children. The moral disorder in David's household arose from unresolved iniquities, a lack of discipline, and a failure to deal with family issues quickly and directly, causing his offspring to suffer spiritually.

Eli and His Sons

Eli was a priest of Israel, but his sons, Hophni and Phinehas, were evil. They misused the priestly office, stealing offerings meant for God, and engaged in immoral behavior, having sex with the women in the sanctuary. (1 Samuel 2:12-17, 22). Despite knowing of their wicked actions, Eli failed to correct or discipline them properly.

Eli's inability to restrain his sons and his passivity led to their downfall and the loss of God's favor on his family. God judged Eli's household, resulting in the death of his sons on the same day (1 Samuel 2:34) and the eventual loss of the priesthood for his lineage (1 Samuel 3:12-14). Eli's failure to spiritually nurture, discipline, and correct his children brought destruction not only to his family but also to Israel, as the Ark of the Covenant was captured by the Philistines (1 Samuel 4:10-22).

Jacob's Dysfunction

Jacob showed favoritism to his son Joseph, which sowed deep jealousy and resentment among his other sons (Genesis 37:3-4). Joseph's brothers, in their jealousy, plotted to kill him but eventually sold him into slavery (Genesis 37:12-28). This act of betrayal tore the family apart for many years.

The dysfunction in Jacob's family led to spiritual and emotional suffering, particularly for Joseph, who was falsely accused, imprisoned, and separated from his family for years (Genesis 39:1-20). His brothers suffered from guilt and shame over their actions, living in deception and fear until they finally faced Joseph again during a time of great famine (Genesis 42-45). Jacob's favoritism and the resulting sibling rivalry created years of spiritual anguish and broken relationships.

Abraham, Sarah, Hagar, and Ishmael

Abraham's family experienced dysfunction due to impatience, frustration, fear, and a lack of trust in God's promise for a child. Unable to conceive, Sarah gave her maidservant Hagar to Abraham, and Hagar gave birth to Ishmael (Genesis 16:1-4). Tension and animosity arose between Sarah and Hagar, leading to envy, jealousy, and strife. When Isaac was born, Sarah demanded that Abraham send Hagar and Ishmael away (Genesis 21:9-10).

This family conflict caused emotional and spiritual turmoil for Ishmael, who was essentially abandoned by his father and cast out into the wilderness (Genesis 21:14-21). Although God provided for Ishmael and promised to make him a great nation, the rift between Isaac and Ishmael's descendants laid the foundation for future spiritual and physical conflict between their lineages present in the world today. (Genesis 16:12; 21:18).

Lot and His Daughters

After fleeing the destruction of Sodom and Gomorrah, Lot's daughters, fearing they would not find husbands, devised a plan to make their father drunk, engage in incest, and have children by him (Genesis 19:30-36). This was a clear example of dysfunction rooted in fear and moral compromise.

The children born from this incestuous relationship became the ancestors of the Moabites and Ammonites, two nations that would later become fierce enemies of Israel and lead the people of God into idolatry (Judges 10:6; 1 Kings 11:5-7). Lot's failure to lead his daughters spiritually, combined with the influence of the morally corrupt culture around them, resulted in disastrous spiritual consequences for future generations.

Isaac and Rebekah's Favoritism

Isaac favoring Esau and Rebekah favoring Jacob created rivalry and deception within their family. Rebekah helped Jacob deceive his father and steal Esau's blessing (Genesis 27:1-29).

The favoritism and deceit fractured the family, leading to years of estrangement between Esau and Jacob. Esau was filled with rage, and Jacob had to flee for his life (Genesis 27:41-45). This deep-rooted family dysfunction caused division and mistrust, leading to spiritual and relational wounds that took years to heal (Genesis 33:1-17).

Dysfunctional Family of Origin: - An Open Gateway for the Spirit of Jezebel

A dysfunctional family environment serves as fertile ground for emotional, psychological, and spiritual vulnerabilities in children, making them prime targets for the influence of the Jezebel spirit. The family is designed by God to be a place of nurture, protection, and stability. Still, when dysfunction infiltrates, it distorts these roles, leaving a void that Jezebel readily exploits to gain a foothold in the lives of children.

In such families, issues like neglect, emotional or physical abuse, rejection, and abandonment often become the norm. These traumatic experiences severely fracture a child's sense of identity, self-worth, and security, driving them to seek validation, comfort, and guidance from external sources—often far removed from godly principles. Jezebel thrives in this chaotic environment where control, manipulation, and a lack of proper nurturing create an opportunity to lure children into destructive behaviors, rebellion, and spiritual deception.

One of the effective ways the Jezebel spirit capitalizes on dysfunction is by magnifying the child's emotional pain, causing them to harbor bitterness, resentment, and unforgiveness toward their parents. Children in dysfunctional families frequently experience deep emotional wounds, whether through rejection, neglect, or constant criticism. These wounds can foster feelings of inadequacy, unworthiness, and shame, which open the door for Jezebel's influence. The spirit whispers lies that distort the child's self-perception and their view of the world. Rather than growing in confidence and security, they are burdened with rejection and abandonment, making them desperate for external validation.

This desperation for acceptance leads them to unhealthy sources— such as toxic friendships, romantic relationships, or online communities that promote rebellion, vanity, and promiscuity, all hallmarks of Jezebel's influence. In this moment of vulnerability, Jezebel implants feelings of worthlessness, anger, and bitterness, driving children further into emotional isolation and rebellion against authority. These destructive behaviors only deepen their wounds, perpetuating a cycle of dysfunction.

Furthermore, the absence of divine order, mainly when fathers are either absent, emotionally detached, or neglectful, creates a spiritual vacuum. Fathers are meant to be protectors, providers, and spiritual leaders, yet in many dysfunctional families, this role is either abandoned or diminished. This void is especially detrimental to sons, who need their father's guidance on their journey toward manhood, and daughters, who require a father's love to affirm their worth. The Jezebel spirit exploits this absence, seeking to emasculate young men and destroy their sense of identity and purpose while leading young girls to seek validation through unhealthy relationships and behaviors.

In cases where fathers neglect their leadership role, Jezebel often raises up a controlling mother to take charge. This creates further distortion as the child's perception of order, leadership, and authority becomes warped. Children in these environments may seek affirmation from even more destructive sources, such as gangs, occult practices, or toxic relationships—areas where Jezebel's influence thrives.

A controlling or dysfunctional mother can also severely undermine a child's emotional and spiritual development by dominating their lives in ways that stunt their autonomy. Rather than providing unconditional love and support, these mothers may impose manipulative or controlling behaviors, fostering an environment of fear and compliance. Jezebel feeds off this imbalance of power, cultivating resentment, rebellion, and confusion in the child, making them more susceptible to the spirit's manipulation.

In families where parents are entangled in cycles of addiction, marital strife, or spiritual apathy, children are left without the spiritual covering they need for protection. The Jezebel spirit quickly fills this void with destructive ideologies, leading children toward a life devoid of God's purpose and direction. When their emotional and spiritual needs go unmet by their family of origin, children become even more vulnerable to Jezebel's influence, making them easy prey for manipulation, control, and false teachings that lead them into spiritual bondage.

Children from dysfunctional families are often drawn toward spiritual deception in their search for meaning and power in a world that feels out of control. Whether through astrology, witchcraft, or the occult, Jezebel thrives on spiritual disorientation, drawing them further from God's truth and deeper into bondage. The lack of spiritual covering leaves children unprotected from demonic attacks and oppression, trapping them in cycles of despair, rebellion, and confusion.

Generational Dysfunction

Dysfunctional family dynamics are often inherited and passed down from generation to generation. Without deliverance, healing, and a renewal of the mind that leads to transformation, the emotional and spiritual wounds inflicted on one generation of children become the same wounds they pass down to their own offspring. This generational cycle of dysfunction is precisely what the Jezebel spirit seeks to perpetuate. By keeping families trapped in patterns of abuse, control, manipulation, and emotional brokenness, Jezebel ensures that future generations remain vulnerable to her destructive influence, continuing the cycle of dysfunction and spiritual oppression.

Children raised in these environments often grow into adults who grapple with co-dependency, narcissism, control issues, or an inability to establish healthy relationships—traits that mirror the characteristics of the Jezebel spirit itself. These individuals, in turn, repeat the same unhealthy patterns they experienced in their upbringing, creating new generations of emotionally wounded and spiritually vulnerable children. This perpetuation of brokenness allows the Jezebel spirit to thrive, fostering environments where emotional pain and spiritual confusion are passed from one generation to the next, like a toxic legacy.

Parents must be willing to confront the dysfunction within their home to break this generational stronghold and close the gateway that allows the Jezebel spirit to maintain influence over the family. This begins with a deep acknowledgment of brokenness and a commitment to seeking healing through counseling, spiritual mentorship, or deliverance. Parents must take responsibility for their own wounds and actively work toward breaking free from the generational cycles of dysfunction that have plagued their family for years if not decades.

Deliverance and healing are not just about addressing past hurts but also about spiritually equipping both parents and children for the future. Parents must reclaim their God-given roles as protectors, nurturers, and spiritual leaders within the home. This requires re-establishing a Christ-centered and Kingdom-focused atmosphere where prayer, sound biblical teaching, compassion, and love prevail. A spiritually healthy family creates a protective covering over its members, fortifying them against the Jezebel spirit's attempts to sow seeds of division, rebellion, and brokenness.

Families can reclaim the spiritual territory that Jezebel has stolen through prayer, deliverance, and intentional spiritual warfare. Parents must engage in warfare on behalf of their children to sever the strongholds from their own past and protect the next generation from falling into the same traps. As parents take ownership of their spiritual authority and lead their children in truth, they model what it means to walk in wholeness and victory, providing their children with the tools to combat Jezebel's schemes.

Ultimately, families must understand that transformation comes from spiritual renewal and the restoration of God's divine order. By addressing the root issues, confronting the dysfunction, and allowing God's healing power to work within the family, parents can help break the generational cycle and restore their children to emotional, psychological, and spiritual wholeness. In doing so, the family becomes a fortress against the Jezebel spirit's influence, a place where future generations can thrive in Christ's love, wisdom, and authority.

Conclusion

As we have seen, the influence of the Jezebel spirit on children in today's society is both pervasive and insidious, working through every available avenue to distort their sense of identity, morality, and purpose. Whether through entertainment, social media, education, or even broken family structures, the Jezebel spirit subtly deceives and manipulates, planting seeds of rebellion, confusion, and self-destruction in the hearts of the next generation. This spirit aims not only to lead children away from biblical truth but also to entrap them in cycles of emotional, psychological, and spiritual bondage that can take years, or even lifetimes, to break.

The stakes are high, and the battle for the hearts and minds of our youth must be taken seriously. Jezebel's influence is not simply about rebellion against authority; it is a strategic attack on the very foundation of a child's identity and relationship with God. Left unchecked, it fosters an environment of chaos, instability, and spiritual blindness, where children are more vulnerable to deception, moral relativism, and emotional wounds that carry into adulthood.

However, this influence is not insurmountable. As parents, educators, spiritual leaders, and members of the body of Christ, we have the power and authority over the spirit of Jezebel. Recognizing Jezebel's tactics is the first step, but beyond awareness, we must actively engage in spiritual warfare to protect our children. This begins at home, where strong foundations of biblical teaching, prayer, and deliverance must be established. Parents must reclaim their roles as spiritual leaders, teaching their children to discern truth from lies and empowering them to walk confidently in their identity in Christ.

Equally important is the church's role, which must rise to the challenge of equipping the next generation to resist the influence of Jezebel. Churches must go beyond entertainment and feel-good messages and return to places where children and youth are taught spiritual warfare, biblical truth, and godly values that counter the cultural tide of deception. By cultivating environments of genuine discipleship, mentorship, and community, we can provide a safe and nurturing space for young people to grow in their faith and find purpose in God's Kingdom.

The influence of Jezebel is not merely a cultural or social issue; it is a spiritual battle for our children's future. And while the challenges are significant, so too is the power of God to bring healing, restoration, and transformation. Through prayer, deliverance, and intentional discipleship, families can break the generational cycles of dysfunction that Jezebel perpetuates and restore their children to emotional, psychological, and spiritual wholeness.

We cannot afford to be passive in this fight. Together, we must stand firm in our calling to protect and guide the next generation, equipping them with the spiritual tools they need to resist the Jezebel spirit's influence and walk confidently in their God-given identity and purpose. In doing so, we prepare them to survive in a world of spiritual darkness and be beacons of light who lead others into the truth and freedom that only Christ can offer.

Chapter Four
How to Protect Children from the Jezebel Spirit

In a world filled with spiritual challenges and temptations, protecting children and youth from the Jezebel spirit requires intentional and active effort. As parents, guardians, and spiritual leaders, we must be vigilant in recognizing the subtle and overt ways this spirit seeks to influence and manipulate the next generation. By equipping our children with spiritual discernment, a strong moral foundation, and an understanding of their identity in Christ, we can guard their hearts and minds against the enemy's schemes. This section provides practical, biblically based strategies for shielding our youth from the destructive influence of the Jezebel spirit.

To combat the Jezebel spirit, it is essential to equip children and adolescents with biblical truth and a strong sense of identity in Christ.

Key strategies include:

1. Teaching and Equipping:

"And how from infancy you have known the Holy Scriptures, which are able to make you wise for salvation through faith in Christ Jesus. All Scripture is God-breathed and is useful for teaching, rebuking, correcting and training in righteousness, so that the servant of God may be thoroughly equipped for every good work" - *2 Timothy 3:15-17*

One of the primary ways to counteract the Jezebel spirit's influence is by ensuring that children have a firm understanding of biblical truth, their identity and authority in Christ, and a solid foundation in deliverance and spiritual warfare. When children know who they are in God's eyes—fearfully and wonderfully made, loved, and protected—they become more resistant to the deception and manipulation of Jezebel.

Parents should encourage consistent Bible study and engage their children with examples of biblical heroes who stood on the side of the Lord and resisted evil influences (e.g., Elijah standing up to Jezebel in 1 Kings and Jehu's command to throw her down). Incorporating scripture memorization is a powerful tool for them to call upon in moments of attack, temptation, or confusion. Helping young people recognize the subtle ways manipulation and perversion manifest, whether through social media, friendships, or family dynamics, is critical. Understanding their authority in Christ and their dominion over demons, specifically Jezebel, helps them recognize when something contradicts God's Word and stand against it.

The Jezebel spirit remains an active force in today's culture, particularly targeting children and adolescents through manipulation, control, perversion, and dysfunction. By drawing on the Word of God and remaining steadfast in prayer and instruction in righteousness, families, churches, and communities can safeguard the next generation from falling prey to this destructive spirit.

"If you're teachable – you're salvageable."

"He guides the humble in what is right and teaches them his way"
- Psalm 25:9

"When pride comes, then comes disgrace, but with humility comes wisdom" - Proverbs 11:2

One of the best ways to remove dysfunction from the home is for parents to model humility and a willingness to learn and grow. The Jezebel spirit often thrives in environments where pride, control, or self-righteousness are present. However, when parents are willing to acknowledge their own mistakes and seek growth, it sets a powerful example for their children.

Parents who are open about their spiritual journey, including their victories and challenges, demonstrate to their children that growth is a continual process. This openness invites God's grace into the home and allows healing to take place where there may have been wounds caused by past dysfunction.

2. Teach Spiritual Warfare and Deliverance Principles

"Praise be to the Lord my Rock, who trains my hands for war, my fingers for battle" - Psalm 144:1

Equip your children with the knowledge of spiritual warfare, including how to recognize and resist the attacks of the enemy. Parents and churches can teach children to use tools like prayer, fasting, and scripture memorization to stand firm in their faith. Teaching them about their authority in Christ empowers them to take an active role in their spiritual defense.

By teaching them about the armor of God (Ephesians 6:10-18), you give them a framework for protecting themselves spiritually. Help them understand that spiritual warfare is not about fear but about standing firm in Christ's authority. Children should learn at an early age how to pray against spiritual attacks and confidently speak the name of Jesus.

Note: Many parents and church leaders hesitate to introduce children and teenagers to the vital teachings of spiritual warfare and deliverance. This reluctance often stems from the pervasive influence of the religious spirit within the modern church, alongside the rise of 'seeker-friendly' environments that prioritize comfort over confronting spiritual truths. This approach is deeply concerning and must be urgently addressed. The spirit of Jezebel, alongside Satan, demons, and spiritual wickedness in high places, thrives in this atmosphere of avoidance, eagerly exploiting youth through subtle yet destructive means. These spiritual forces do not discriminate by age; in fact, they often prefer to target children at their most vulnerable stages, beginning as early as elementary school and sometimes even earlier.

Failing to equip our youth for spiritual warfare leaves them exposed to the enemy's attacks, often without the knowledge or tools to defend themselves. It is imperative that churches, parents, and Christian leaders recognize that spiritual battles are not confined to adulthood. Demonic forces are waging war on our children, and ignoring this reality only strengthens their hold.

For those parents, churches, and Christian leaders who may feel unprepared in the area of spiritual warfare and deliverance ministry, we, the authors, strongly encourage you to seek assistance and guidance. Our ministry is here to help equip you with the knowledge and tools necessary to protect the next generation from these relentless spiritual attacks. Together, we can ensure our children are not left defenseless in this critical fight for their souls.

"Finally, be strong in the Lord and in his mighty power. Put on the full armor of God, so that you can take your stand against the devil's schemes" - Ephesians 6:10-11

"Parents and children must be thoroughly equipped in spiritual warfare and deliverance to effectively defend themselves against the Jezebel spirit's calculated attacks and deceptive schemes. The Jezebel spirit operates subtly, infiltrating families, institutions, and individual minds through manipulation, deception, and control. Without a solid understanding of spiritual warfare, families are left exposed and defenseless, often unaware of the spirit's influence or how to resist its advances.

It is crucial for parents to first seek spiritual deliverance for any wounds, traumas, or unresolved issues in their own lives that may have created openings for the Jezebel spirit to operate. By addressing these vulnerabilities and renouncing any sinful behaviors or toxic influences, they can break free from the spirit's hold and fortify themselves against future attacks. This process strengthens their personal walk with Christ and sets a powerful example for their children.

Parents must actively teach their children the principles of spiritual warfare, beginning with daily prayers for protection over their minds, hearts, and spirits. Leading family prayers that specifically seek deliverance from the influence of the Jezebel spirit creates a spiritual covering over the household, inviting God's protection and presence into their home. Additionally, parents should emphasize the importance of their children's identity in Christ, teaching them the authority they have as believers. When children understand their spiritual authority, they are empowered to stand firm against any spiritual attacks, knowing they are not powerless.

By instilling these spiritual disciplines early on, families can develop strong spiritual resilience, recognizing and resisting the Jezebel spirit's subtle tactics before they take root. Together, through intentional prayer, deliverance, and instruction, families can build a fortified defense against the forces of darkness seeking to undermine their faith and unity."

3. Engaging in Spiritual Warfare and Deliverance

"For though we live in the world, we do not wage war as the world does. The weapons we fight with are not the weapons of the world. On the contrary, they have divine power to demolish strongholds" - 2 Corinthians 10:3-4

Active engagement in Spiritual warfare and deliverance is mandatory. This involves but is not limited to, prayer, eradication of demonic spirits, breaking of strongholds that have taken hold on the child's life, and spiritual guidance to assist the child in addressing mental and emotional trauma that developed. It is imperative to restore the child's emotional and spiritual well-being through healing and deliverance.

Deliverance is a key component of spiritual warfare, especially when dealing with strongholds that have already taken root. Parents must not only seek deliverance for themselves but also actively pray for their children's deliverance from any generational curses, emotional wounds, or spiritual influences they may have unknowingly allowed into their lives. The Jezebel spirit often gains a foothold through trauma, rejection, or persistent sin, and deliverance is necessary to break these chains. Whether through prayer, fasting, or partnering with experienced spiritual leaders, families can experience true freedom when they confront and expel the influence of the Jezebel spirit.

Deliverance is a critical aspect of spiritual protection. The Jezebel spirit often takes hold through emotional wounds, past trauma, or repeated exposure to ungodly influences. Parents need to be aware of these openings and seek deliverance for their children and themselves to break free from spiritual bondage. Deliverance helps remove the Jezebel spirit's foothold in the family, allowing healing and restoration to take place.

It is equally important for families to remain aware of the continual nature of spiritual warfare. Parents are encouraged to cultivate active discernment, teaching their children how to recognize spiritual attacks. The Jezebel spirit often works through subtle tactics like division, jealousy, pride, and rebellion. Helping children identify these tactics equips them to resist manipulation, whether it comes from peers, media, or even their thoughts and emotions. By instilling biblical values and teaching children to rely on the Holy Spirit for wisdom, parents can help them discern truth from lies. Proverbs 22:6 says, "Train up a child in the way he should go, and when he is old, he will not depart from it." This training is not just intellectual but deeply spiritual.

The Jezebel spirit is relentless and systematic in its attacks, seeking to exploit weaknesses over time. Therefore, parents and children must stay engaged in spiritual disciplines, continually fortifying themselves against new schemes and influences. This includes regular prayer, studying God's Word, and maintaining a solid connection with a community of believers who can provide support and accountability.

Families can build strong spiritual foundations that protect against the Jezebel spirit's attacks by teaching and modeling spiritual warfare and deliverance. They can also begin to reclaim their authority in Christ, recognizing that they have the power to resist the enemy's schemes through the strength of the Holy Spirit. Encouraging this proactive approach equips both parents and children to stand firm against spiritual manipulation, ensuring that the Jezebel spirit does not gain a foothold in their lives.

Parents play a key role in modeling spiritual warfare and deliverance. They must be vigilant in protecting their homes, leading by example in prayer, fasting, and seeking God's wisdom. When parents are spiritually equipped, they can recognize the subtle ways the Jezebel spirit tries to infiltrate the family, such as through division, rebellion, or emotional manipulation. They can then take proactive steps to address these issues before they grow into more significant spiritual strongholds.

As the Jezebel spirit operates through deception, control, and manipulation, it systematically targets families, particularly children, because they are vulnerable and still forming their spiritual and emotional identities. Without proper spiritual training, both parents and children are at a higher risk of falling prey to these attacks.

Additionally, it's essential for parents to develop a deep understanding of the spiritual authority they have in Christ. Scripture tells us that believers are seated with Christ in heavenly places, with authority over all spiritual forces of evil.

I have given you authority to trample on snakes and scorpions
and to overcome all the power of the enemy; nothing will harm you -
Luke 10:19

Parents must exercise this authority through prayer, declaring protection and freedom over their children. They should diligently pray for their children's minds, hearts, and environments—asking God to guard them against the influences of the Jezebel spirit in their schools, media consumption, friendships, and even within religious settings where false teachings may be present.

Ultimately, the goal of spiritual warfare and deliverance is not just defense but victory. Jesus has already won the ultimate victory on the cross, and believers are called to walk in that victory by resisting the devil and his schemes. Through intentional spiritual discipline and awareness, families can live in freedom from the influence of the Jezebel spirit. When parents and children are armed with spiritual knowledge and practical tools, they can resist deception, break free from bondage, and grow in their relationship with Christ.

4. Prophetic Exhortation

"But the one who prophesies speaks to people for their
strengthening, encouraging and comfort" - 1 Corinthians 14:3

In modern-day prophetic ministry, the focus on edifying, encouraging, and comforting the youth should be imparted correctly to assist in their deliverance, healing, and wholeness and provide essential protection from the Jezebel spirit in several ways.

Edification - Prophetic words and teachings that build up a child's faith and identity in Christ serve as a safeguard against the Jezebel

149

spirit's tactics. When children are equipped with a strong sense of their spiritual value and purpose, they are less vulnerable to the deception and manipulation associated with this spirit. The prophetic ministry can help foster a sense of belonging and self-worth rooted in God's truth, countering the lies of rejection and insecurity that Jezebel often uses to attack youth.

Exhortation - Encouraging children to walk in God's ways, maintain purity, and avoid harmful influences is vital in keeping them spiritually protected. Prophetic ministries emphasizing practical applications of biblical principles can guide children to recognize and reject ungodly behaviors and choices. This helps develop discernment, allowing them to identify and resist the subtle and overt influences of the Jezebel spirit in their daily lives.

Comfort - The Jezebel spirit often attacks children through fear, intimidation, or emotional trauma. Prophetic ministries that offer comfort, reassurance, and healing provide a spiritual refuge for children, helping them recover from wounds caused by dysfunctional family environments, societal pressures, or other negative experiences. Comforting prophetic words can reaffirm God's protection and love, helping children feel secure and cared for and reducing the spirit's ability to exploit feelings of vulnerability or abandonment.

By incorporating these spiritual elements in deliverance, prophetic ministry becomes a powerful tool in reinforcing a child's spiritual foundation, creating a protective barrier that shields them from the influence of the Jezebel spirit. Strengthening the child through words of encouragement involves reinforcing positive self-identity. Comforting words have a calming effect and foster an internal environment of peace, safety, and security.

Parents and leaders can rely on prophetic insights and operations to recognize early signs of spiritual attacks and, intervene with timely words of encouragement, and dismantle the negative effects of trauma and the Jezebel spirit's influence.

5. Limit Exposure to Harmful Media and Environments

"I will not look with approval on anything that is vile. I hate what faithless people do; I will have no part in it" - *Psalm 101:3*

The Jezebel spirit often works through modern media, promoting vanity, rebellion, immorality, and violence. Being intentional about what children consume can reduce exposure to these harmful influences. Monitor the music, movies, social media platforms, and games your children engage with. Discuss the content they consume and help them critically assess whether it aligns with biblical values or not. While it's important not to be controlling, educating them about the potential spiritual dangers behind certain media can help them make informed decisions themselves. Providing alternatives, such as faith-based content, healthy entertainment, and activities that promote creativity, physical engagement, and connection with the outdoors, can redirect their focus to better environments.

6. Addressing Family Dysfunction

There are many practical and spiritual ways for parents to create a healthier environment where their children can break free from the influence of the Jezebel spirit and remove dysfunction from the home. The home environment plays a critical role in shaping a child's emotional and spiritual development, and eliminating dysfunction is crucial in preventing the Jezebel spirit from gaining a foothold.

Establish a Christ-Centered Household

One of the most important steps parents can take is to ensure that Christ is at the center of their home. This involves creating an environment where the Kingdom of God and His Righteousness are prioritized through Bible study, family prayer, and worship.

But seek first the kingdom of God and His righteousness, and all these things shall be added to you – Matthew 6:33

When children see their parents actively pursuing the Kingdom of God and live a life of obedience and devotion to Christ, it models a healthy spiritual life. Following the leading and guiding of the Holy Spirit in every aspect of the home makes it difficult for the Jezebel spirit to operate, as the focus is on God's authority and truth.

Parents should also encourage personal spiritual growth for their children. Teaching children how to pray, read scripture, exercise authority over the demonic, and listen to the Holy Spirit helps them to walk in dominion and form a solid personal relationship with God, empowering them to resist deception and manipulation from external forces.

Train up a child in the way he should go, and when he is old, he will not depart from it – Proverbs 22:6

Create Open Communication and Emotional Safety

"These commandments that I give you today are to be on your hearts. Impress them on your children. Talk about them when you sit

at home and when you walk along the road, when you lie down and when you get up." Deuteronomy 6:6-7

Dysfunction in a home often arises when communication breaks down or when children don't feel emotionally secure. Parents need to establish an environment of trust and open dialogue where children feel free to express their emotions, ask questions, and discuss any struggles they face without fear of judgment. Parents need to refrain from being critical, demeaning, and judgmental towards their children, or else they run the risk of the child 'shutting down.' By adopting emotional safety, parents create a space where children are less likely to turn to external influences like the Jezebel spirit for comfort, validation, or guidance.

Emotional parental availability can break the cycle of control and manipulation that the Jezebel spirit thrives on. When children feel loved, heard, and understood, they are more emotionally resilient and less vulnerable to external manipulative forces.

Lead by Example

"In everything set them an example by doing what is good. In your teaching show integrity, seriousness." – Titus 2:7

Children often imitate the relational dynamics they see at home. If parents exhibit controlling, manipulative, or toxic behaviors, children are more likely to internalize those patterns and become vulnerable to the influence of the Jezebel spirit. Therefore, parents should strive to model healthy relationships characterized by mutual respect, love, and godly authority.

Parents should take responsibility for their own emotional and spiritual health, seeking counseling or mentorship if needed to address unresolved issues or trauma that could lead to dysfunction and toxic Jezebelic behaviors. Demonstrating humility, repentance, faith, and forgiveness sets a powerful example for children and prevents the spirit of Jezebel from exploiting areas of unresolved conflict or emotional wounds.

Break Generational Patterns of Dysfunction

"The one who sins is the one who will die. The child will not share the guilt of the parent, nor will the parent share the guilt of the child. The righteousness of the righteous will be credited to them, and the wickedness of the wicked will be charged against them" - Ezekiel 18:20

The Jezebel spirit often operates through generational patterns of dysfunction, such as addiction, abuse, control, and neglect. Parents need to recognize and break these patterns by acknowledging past trauma or negative behaviors that may have been passed down through the family. Seeking deliverance, engaging in spiritual warfare, and taking intentional steps to heal from past wounds are crucial for breaking these strongholds.

Through prayer and deliverance ministry, parents can remove any spiritual footholds that the Jezebel spirit may have in their family. By addressing the root causes of dysfunction, parents free their children from being affected by the same patterns of brokenness.

Establish Clear Boundaries and Discipline

"Whoever spares the rod hates their children, but the one who loves their children is careful to discipline them" – Proverbs 13:24

"No discipline seems pleasant at the time, but painful. Later on, however, it produces a harvest of righteousness and peace for those who have been trained by it." – Hebrews 12:11

Children need boundaries to feel secure and understand healthy limits. A lack of boundaries or inconsistent discipline can lead to confusion, rebellion, and emotional instability, areas where the Jezebel spirit can gain influence. Parents should establish clear, consistent rules that are enforced with love, not control. Biblical principles should guide discipline, emphasizing correction as an act of love, not punishment out of anger or frustration.

Healthy boundaries also apply to what is allowed into the home, such as media, music, and entertainment. Parents must be vigilant in protecting their children from content that glorifies rebellion, promiscuity, or other influences linked to the Jezebel spirit. Creating boundaries in this area teaches children to discern what aligns with God's truth.

Encourage Positive Friendships and Mentorships

"Walk with the wise and become wise, for a companion of fools suffers harm." – Proverbs 13:20

"Do not be misled: 'Bad company corrupts good character.'" 1 Corinthians 15:33

Ensuring that positive, godly influences surround children can help counteract the manipulative influence of the Jezebel spirit. Parents should encourage their children to seek healthy friendships and Christian mentors who can offer support, encouragement, and accountability. These relationships can serve as a spiritual and emotional buffer, helping children develop strong connections that align with God's values.

Youth groups, Christian camps, and church communities can provide positive peer influence and a sense of belonging. When children feel accepted and loved within a godly community, they are less likely to seek validation from toxic sources.

Release a Spirit of Forgiveness and Repentance

"Be kind and compassionate to one another, forgiving each other, just as in Christ God forgave you." - Ephesians 4:32

Unforgiveness is a powerful tool that the Jezebel spirit uses to create division and dysfunction within families. Parents should lead by example, fostering a spirit of forgiveness in the home. This means apologizing when wrong and teaching children the importance of forgiving others. Forgiveness breaks the power of bitterness, resentment, and division, creating an atmosphere of unity and love where the Jezebel spirit cannot thrive.

"If we confess our sins, he is faithful and just and will forgive us our sins and purify us from all unrighteousness." – I John 1:9

Repentance is equally important. When parents are willing to repent for past mistakes and actively seek to change, they demonstrate humility and openness to God's transformative power. This openness invites healing into the home and establishes a spiritual foundation where the Jezebel spirit has no place.

Dysfunction often arises from unresolved conflicts and unforgiveness within the family. The Jezebel spirit thrives on division and bitterness, using them to sow discord and create emotional barriers. Parents must lead the way in practicing forgiveness and reconciliation within their marriage and with their children.

Teaching children how to forgive others and seek reconciliation is essential for creating a peaceful home. When forgiveness becomes a regular practice, it prevents bitterness from taking root and neutralizes one of the key tactics of the Jezebel spirit—using past hurts to create division.

Promote Individual Identity in Christ

"For in him we live, and move, and have our being; as certain also of your own poets have said, For we are also his offspring". –
Acts 17:28

One of the most effective ways to combat the Jezebel spirit's influence is by reinforcing each family member's identity in Christ. The Jezebel spirit seeks to manipulate by distorting a child's sense of worth, purpose, and identity. Parents can counter this by regularly affirming their children's value as sons and daughters of God, teaching them that their worth comes from being loved by God, not from external validation or performance.

"But he who is joined to the Lord becomes one spirit with him" - I Corinthians 6:17

"For you died, and your life is now hidden with Christ in God." - Colossians 3:3

Encourage children to discover their God-given gifts and talents, fostering a sense of purpose rooted in their relationship with God. Helping children build a strong spiritual foundation from a young age equips them to reject the lies of the Jezebel spirit that attempt to undermine their sense of identity.

Address and Heal Emotional Wounds

Many times, the Jezebel spirit capitalizes on emotional wounds, using past trauma, rejection, or unresolved pain to manipulate and control. Parents should proactively identify emotional wounds that may exist within the family, particularly in their children. Emotional healing is a key step in freeing children from the stronghold of the Jezebel spirit.

Parents should create an environment where children feel safe to express their feelings and struggles without fear of judgment or punishment. They can also help their children by seeking pastoral counseling, therapy, or deliverance ministry, which provides a path for inner healing. By dealing with emotional wounds head-on, parents close the door to the Jezebel spirit's attempts to exploit their child's pain.

Exemplify Christ in your marriage

"Husbands, love your wives, just as Christ loved the church and gave himself up for her." - Ephesians 5:25

"Wives, submit yourselves to your own husbands as you do to the Lord. For the husband is the head of the wife as Christ is the head of the church, his body, of which he is the Savior." - Ephesians 5:22-23

The relationship between parents is central to the home's spiritual health. A healthy, loving marriage that reflects mutual respect and godly principles provides stability and security for children. However, when marital dysfunction, such as unresolved conflict, control, or emotional neglect, exists, it creates an environment where the Jezebel spirit can enter and cause strife and division.

"Husbands, in the same way be considerate as you live with your wives, and treat them with respect as the weaker partner and as heirs with you of the gracious gift of life, so that nothing will hinder your prayers." – I Peter 3:7

Parents should value their marriage, investing time in building a strong partnership based on biblical values. Seeking marriage coaching when necessary, resolving conflicts through obedience to the Word, engaging in healthy communication, and working together as a team to lead the family spiritually are all vital steps. When children witness their parents operating in unity, it models healthy relationships, sets a spiritual tone for the entire household, and shuts the door to the Jezebel spirit.

159

Guard the Home from Toxic Influences

"Be alert and of sober mind. Your enemy the devil prowls around like a roaring lion looking for someone to devour." - 1 Peter 5:8

"Above all else, guard your heart, for everything you do flows from it." - Proverbs 4:23

In today's culture, many harmful influences can enter the home through media, social interactions, or entertainment. The Jezebel spirit uses these vehicles to promote rebellion, sexual immorality, self-idolatry, and other destructive behaviors. Parents need to be vigilant about what they permit into their homes.

Of course, this doesn't mean creating a rigid or overly restrictive environment but rather one that promotes discernment. Parents should actively monitor what media their children consume, whether television, music, social media, or video games. Encouraging children to think critically and spiritually about the content they engage with and how it aligns with Kingdom values helps them develop the skills to resist negative influences on their own.

Having open conversations about the messages behind media content and its potential spiritual impact teaches children to recognize the subtle ways the Jezebel spirit works to influence their thoughts and behavior.

7. Accountability and Support

Accountability is crucial in maintaining a spiritual walk and resisting the influence of the Jezebel spirit. Parents can create accountability within the family by encouraging open and honest communication and healthy correction. Regular family discussions about spiritual challenges, temptations, struggles, and victories create a supportive environment where each member feels encouraged to share and learn.

Furthermore, being part of a quality church body that emphasizes the spiritual laws, deliverance principles, and values of the Kingdom of God helps reinforce spiritual accountability at home. Encouraging children to participate in youth groups, Bible studies, or discipleship programs allows them to form positive connections with godly mentors who can provide accountability. Parents should also have trusted spiritual mentors or accountability partners with whom they can share their challenges and seek counsel.

8. Seek Professional Help When Necessary

"Where no counsel is, the people fall: But in the multitude of counsellors there is safety" – Proverbs 11:14

If the dysfunction in a home is severe—such as in cases of abuse, addiction, or deep emotional wounds, parents should seek professional counseling, coaching, or therapy. There is no shame in seeking outside help to address family issues. In doing so, parents demonstrate that healing, deliverance, and restoration are priorities. A willingness to work through dysfunction with the help of those who are spiritually discerning and professionally trained can break the cycle of toxic behavior that the Jezebel spirit often exploits.

Parents play a crucial role in safeguarding their children from the influence of the Jezebel spirit by creating a spiritually vibrant and emotionally healthy home environment. Through establishing a household that focuses on God and His Kingdom, nurturing healthy relationships, addressing emotional wounds, and practicing spiritual warfare, families can break free from dysfunction and resist the schemes of the Jezebel spirit. By leading with love, humility, and spiritual authority, parents set the tone for their children's spiritual freedom and resilience, creating a home where God's truth and grace reign.

Conclusion

As we recognize the pervasive influence of the Jezebel spirit on today's youth, it is clear that this is not merely a battle over behavior or societal norms—it is a spiritual war for the very souls, identities, and futures of our children. The Jezebel spirit seeks to undermine their God-given purpose, distort their understanding of truth, and entrap them in cycles of rebellion, emotional instability, and spiritual confusion. Yet, God has equipped us with spiritual weapons and authority to stand against these attacks, and by engaging in spiritual warfare and deliverance, we can safeguard the next generation and lead them into the fullness of their divine calling.

Central to protecting children and adolescents from the Jezebel spirit is the understanding that this battle must be fought on a spiritual level. Parents and spiritual leaders are not just caretakers of physical and emotional well-being but must also take on the role of spiritual warriors. This requires actively engaging in spiritual warfare on behalf of our children—through prayer, fasting, and the intentional use of God's Word to combat the lies and deception that the Jezebel spirit seeks to implant in their hearts and minds. Families must establish a foundation of consistent, fervent prayer, covering their children in God's protection and standing against the spiritual forces that seek to ensnare them.

Spiritual warfare goes beyond just daily prayer; it involves identifying and dismantling the strongholds that the Jezebel spirit attempts to set up in the lives of children. Whether it is rebellion, confusion about their identity, or an attraction to worldly values, these strongholds must be confronted head-on through the power of the Holy Spirit. Parents must be equipped to discern when their children are under spiritual attack and take authority over these influences, using the spiritual tools provided to them by God. Teaching children to stand firm in the Word, pray, and speak life over themselves are vital skills in helping them resist the temptations and deceptions that Jezebel uses to draw them away from God.

In addition to spiritual warfare, deliverance ministry plays a crucial role in setting children and adolescents free from the grip of the Jezebel spirit. The Jezebel spirit seeks to attach itself to areas of emotional wounding, unresolved trauma, or generational dysfunction within a family. Deliverance ministry works to break these chains by confronting demonic influences and removing any legal ground they may have over a child's life. Parents must seek deliverance for their own wounds, traumas, and spiritual baggage to ensure they are not inadvertently passing these issues down to their children. The healing of parents is foundational to breaking generational cycles of dysfunction that Jezebel often exploits.

Through deliverance, parents and children can experience spiritual freedom and healing, allowing them to close the doors Jezebel uses to gain influence. Whether these doors have been opened through rebellion, unforgiveness, trauma, or exposure to ungodly influences, deliverance ministry brings a powerful release from bondage. Families need to understand that deliverance is not a one-time event but an ongoing process of cleansing and renewal, ensuring that their hearts and homes are aligned with God's Kingdom.

The church also has a vital role to play in this battle. Church leaders and ministries must rise to the challenge of equipping parents and young people with the knowledge and tools needed to engage in spiritual warfare and deliverance. Youth ministries, in particular, should focus on educating our youth about the reality of spiritual warfare, teaching them to recognize the Jezebel spirit's tactics, and showing them how to stand firm in their authority in Christ and how to cast out demons. By incorporating deliverance ministry into the regular life of the church, we provide a way for individuals to break free from the spiritual oppression that often goes unaddressed in many Christian circles.

The entertainment-driven culture of many youth ministries must be replaced with an emphasis on biblical teaching, prayer, and practical training in spiritual warfare. Empowering young people to confront the spiritual forces at work in their lives is one of the most effective ways to inoculate them against Jezebel's influence. Rather than viewing spiritual warfare and deliverance as extreme or rare occurrences, we must normalize these practices as part of the daily Christian walk. When children and adolescents are equipped with the understanding that they are engaged in a spiritual battle and that they have the power and authority through Christ to resist the enemy, they can walk in greater spiritual maturity and discernment.

Ultimately, protecting children and adolescents from the Jezebel spirit requires a combined effort of spiritual warfare, deliverance, and discipleship. This battle is not just about keeping them safe from cultural influences—it is about empowering them to thrive in the fullness of their God-given identity and purpose. The enemy's agenda to steal, kill, and destroy can be thwarted when parents, churches, and communities rise up as spiritual protectors, covering their children in prayer, equipping them with biblical truth, and leading them through deliverance from any bondage or deception.

The Jezebel spirit's influence is great, but God's power is greater. Through the weapons of spiritual warfare, the ministry of deliverance, and the power of discipleship, families can break the generational cycles of dysfunction, rebellion, and confusion and restore their children to emotional, psychological, and spiritual wholeness. As we stand united in this spiritual battle, we prepare a generation to not only resist Jezebel's influence but to become leaders in God's Kingdom, equipped to carry His truth and light to a world in need.

The next generation is under siege, but the Word of God has empowered us to dismantle Jezebel's stronghold and lead them to a place of victory.

Chapter Five
Prayers of Deliverance for Children

The following pages provide a collection of specific prayers that can be declare over your children, each designed to address various spiritual needs and situations. These prayers are not only meant to be spoken by parents on behalf of their children but can also be used by children as a powerful tool in their own spiritual journey. We strongly encourage that, where appropriate, children speak these prayers out loud themselves, as there is great power in them learning to use their own voice to resist the enemy and affirm their identity in Christ.

However, it is important to note that not all prayers may be suitable for every age group. For younger children, we recommend that parents' guide them through the prayers, assisting with language or concepts they may not fully understand. This practice not only helps instill the habit of prayer in children but also fosters spiritual bonding between parent and child. For older children and teenagers, these prayers can serve as a way for them to develop spiritual maturity, learning to take personal authority over their lives in prayer.

As you engage in these prayers together, remember that the words spoken carry the weight of faith and authority. Parents, take the opportunity to explain the meaning behind each prayer, allowing children to understand the spiritual significance of what they are declaring. In doing so, you not only help protect your child but also equip them with the knowledge and tools they need to grow strong in their faith and in their ability to stand against spiritual attacks. These prayers are meant to be more than recitations; they are declarations of God's power and promises over the lives of your children, helping them to walk in the freedom and protection that Christ has already secured for them.

General Prayer

Heavenly Father, reveal to me any areas in my life where the Jezebel spirit has gained influence and a demonic stronghold. Help me discern manipulation, pride, or idolatry, and lead me to surrender these things to You. I renounce all forms of control and self-glorification and ask for the grace to walk in humility and truth.

Father, in the name of Jesus I repent from permitting the Jezebel spirit to influence my life. I ask you to forgive me for my association with her network, eunuchs and children. I repent of all idolatry, the lusts of the flesh and all areas of rebellion.

Jezebel, you are defeated. You no longer rule my life. Every assignment against me is canceled out. Every door and access point are closed. I stand boldly against you in the name of Jesus. I bind up the ruling spirit of Jezebel in the unseen realm.

I break the curse of Jezebel going back to ten generations on both sides of my family bloodline. Jezebels control and demonic attacks stop now! I cut, sever, break and destroy all cords, snares, fetters, chains and weapons of control used by this evil network.

All spirits tied to Jezebel, including manipulation, control, Queen of Heaven, Queen of Babylon, hatred of men, anger towards father, rebellion towards husband, male authority, God, the untamed tongue, temper, destruction of the family, women liberation spirits have no power over me.

I break all manipulation, lies, denial, and deception caused by the spirit of Jezebel.

I rebuke all spirits of false teaching and false prophecy connected to Jezebel. I break the powers of every word curse and words of witchcraft spoken against my life by the spirit of Jezebel operating in people close to me.

Father, protect me from the temptations of this world and empower me to seek only Your will. In Jesus' name, Amen.

Prayer regarding Social Media

Lord, I ask for wisdom and discernment in my use of social media. I willfully detach myself from Jezebel's digital playground. Guard my heart against vanity, comparison, and the desire for validation from others. Help me to use social media platforms responsibly and in ways that honor You, promote the Kingdom of Heaven and inspire those around me. Father, help me to seek my worth in You only, and not in the approval of others. No longer will I be a people pleaser, but rather a God pleaser. Holy Spirit teach me to be content in the Father's love and identity. In Jesus' name, Amen.

Prayer regarding Self-Worship and Idolatry of Self

Lord, Forgive me for any ways in which I have placed myself, my desires, my ambitions or my accomplishments above You. Expose the ways in which I have stumbled into self-worship and idolatry of self, and places where I have sought validation, power, or identity independent from You.

I repent of pride, self-centeredness, and any vain pursuit of worldly praise. I renounce any beliefs or behaviors that have exalted my own will over Your perfect will. Remind me, Lord, that my value comes from being Your beloved child, not from what I achieve or how others perceive me.

Break down any idols I've unknowingly built in my heart that have taken Your place. Help me to live in humility, recognizing that You are the source of all good things in my life. May I reflect Your glory, not my own. Teach me to find true satisfaction in Your love and not in self-promotion or worldly success.

Help me to surrender my life to You fully and to trust in Your plan. Teach me to live humbly and to serve others selflessly. Break the stronghold of self-idolatry in my life and lead me in the path of righteousness and humility. In Jesus' name, Amen.

Toxic Relationships and Connections

Lord, I ask for healing and restoration in my relationships, both with family members, friends, church family and classmates. Where there is control, manipulation, intimidation and dominance, let Your light and truth overpower these evil weapons of destruction. Give me the strength to set healthy boundaries and to seek relationships that honor You. I ask for wisdom in discerning toxic influences, and I renounce all forms of manipulation and control in my life. Holy Spirit, each me to love others as God love me, with kindness, honesty, and humility. In Jesus' name, Amen.

Prayer regarding Narcissistic Leadership and ungodly Authority

Lord, I recognize that all authority comes from You, but I also recognize that not all leaders walk in Your ways. Forgive me if I have allowed myself to be influenced by ungodly authority or have submitted to leadership that exalts self over You.

I pray for any narcissistic and Jezebelic leadership that may be over my life—leaders who seek their own gain, who abuse their power, and lead with pride and selfish ambition. I ask for Your protection over my heart and mind from their influence. Shield me from manipulation, control, and the spirit of pride that may operate through them. Give me discernment to distinguish when authority is being used for selfish purposes rather than for Your glory and the advancement of Your Kingdom.

Father, where I have been wounded by ungodly authority, I ask for Your healing. Free me from any fear, bitterness, resentment or rage that may have taken root because of past or present experiences. Help me to walk in forgiveness and trust that You are the ultimate authority in my life.

Give me the wisdom to navigate these situations with wisdom, love and Your word. Show me areas where I might need to distance myself from any toxic leadership while remaining in alignment with Your will for my life. Direct me to godly mentors, coaches and leaders who will guide me according to Your truth.

Spiritual Warfare - Overcoming the Jezebel Spirit

Lord Jesus, I acknowledge Your power and authority over all things. I lift up my heart, my life, my family and friends to You, seeking deliverance from the Jezebel spirit, which seeks to manipulate, control, and destroy Your people.

In the name of Jesus, I renounce and reject all influence of the Jezebel spirit over my life, my home, and my relationships. I break every tie and foothold this spirit has tried to establish, and I declare that it has no power or authority over me. By the authority given to me through the name of Jesus, I bind the Jezebel spirit and all spirits that work with it, and I command them to leave now, In Jesus name.

Lord, I ask that You open my eyes to any ways this spirit may be working in my life or around me. Expose every tactic, scheme, plot and deception that seeks to undermine my walk with You, my identity in Christ, and the purposes You have for my life. Let Your truth and light be abundant in every area of my life and give me discernment to recognize the works of this insidious spirit.

I declare and decree that I will not bow down to manipulation, intimidation, or fear. I reject the spirit of control and domination that seeks to silence the voice of God in my life.

Have me to stand firm in the faith, knowing that You have given me authority to tread on serpents and scorpions and over all the power of the enemy.

I pray for protection over my mind, emotions, and spirit. Guard my thoughts from the lies and confusion that this spirit tries to bring. Strengthen me to walk in cleanliness, humility, and obedience to Your Word, refusing to be swayed by the influences of lust of the flesh, the lust of the eyes and the pride of life.

Father, thank You for the victory that is already mine in Christ Jesus. I stand firm in the promises of your word, knowing that You fight for me and that no spirit of darkness can prevail against Your power. Thank you, Lord, for delivering me. In Jesus' mighty name, Amen.

Restoring Identity stolen from the Jezebel Spirit

Heavenly Father, You are the source of my identity. You created me with purpose. You have given me a unique identity that reflects Your image. Today, I seek deliverance for every part of my identity that has been stolen, distorted, or manipulated by the Jezebel spirit. I acknowledge that the enemy, through the Jezebel spirit, has sought to steal my sense of worth, purpose, and confidence.

But today I stand on Your Word, which states that the enemy is defeated, and I have dominion over demons and authority over evil spirits, including Jezebel. I declare that everything that the spirit of Jezebel has stolen from me—spiritually, emotionally, and mentally, be returned seven-fold.

I renounce every lie that has been spoken over my life by the Jezebel spirit, and I break the power of any deception that has taken root in my mind. I reject the false identities, insecurities, and confusion that have tried to take hold of me. I declare that my identity is not defined by the words, opinions, or manipulations of others, but by You, my Father. I am who You say I am.

Father, I ask that You restore my identity to its completeness. Restore the confidence, peace, and joy that have been stripped away.

Heal any wounds that have caused me to doubt who I am in Christ No longer will I allow fear and rejection to mold me.

I rebuke the spirit of manipulation, control, and domination that has attempted to confuse and sabotage me. I retrieve the gifts, callings, dreams, treasure and talent that You have placed in me. I declare that the Jezebel spirit has no authority over my life, my mind, or my future. I command it to leave now, in the name of Jesus.

Holy Spirit, repair and fill every area of my life where the Jezebel spirit once operated. Restore my ability to hear Your voice clearly and walk in the freedom that comes from being led by the Holy Spirit. I declare that I am free from the chains of confusion, doubt, guilt, shame and fear. I am free to be the person You created me to be.

Father, thank You for the complete restoration of my identity. I know that I am loved, valued, loved and called according to Your purpose. In Jesus' name, Amen.

Final Prayer of Freedom from Jezebel's Influence and Control

Heavenly Father, I thank You for the truth revealed through Your Word. I surrender my heart, my mind, and life to You totally. I ask for Your direction as I walk in freedom from the influence of the Jezebel spirit and narcissism. Equip me and strengthen me to resist the temptations of this world system and to live a Holy life that honors You. Help me to reflect Your character and Your love in my relationships, and in the daily decisions I have to make. I declare that my identity is found in You alone, and I am no longer entangled in Jezebels web of destruction. In Jesus' name, Amen.

Other Books by Robert & Dixie Summers

Deliverance Training Manual - 101©

Deliverance Training Manual 201 ©

Genuine Fathers – Willing Sons ©

Kingdom Principles of Success, Wealth & Prosperity ©

Gossip – The Weapon of Mass Destruction ©

Harboring the Spirit of Jezebel ©

Throw Jezebel Down ©

Jezebels Whoredoms, Perversions and Witchcrafts ©

The Petrified Soul ©

No More – No Mas ©

Enough ©

Overcoming Financial Dysfunction ©

For Professional Life Transformation Coaching please call (877) 985-1744 or visit www.icanadvance.com

For more information regarding products and ministry please visit summersministries.com

Made in the USA
Columbia, SC
11 October 2024